Pablo Neruda

T0345583

Titles in the series Critical Lives present the work of leading cultural figures of the modern period. Each book explores the life of the artist, writer, philosopher or architect in question and relates it to their major works.

Jean Genet Stephen Barber	Georges Bataille Stuart Kendall
Michel Foucault David Macey	Ludwig Wittgenstein Edward Kanterian
Pablo Picasso Mary Ann Caws	Frank Lloyd Wright Robert McCarter
Franz Kafka Sander L. Gilman	Octavio Paz Nick Caistor
Guy Debord Andy Merrifield	Walter Benjamin Esther Leslie
Marcel Duchamp Caroline Cros	Charles Baudelaire Rosemary Lloyd
James Joyce Andrew Gibson	Jean Cocteau James S. Williams
Frank Lloyd Wright Robert McCarter	Sergei Eisenstein Mike O'Mahony
Jean-Paul Sartre Andrew Leak	Salvador Dalí Mary Ann Caws
Noam Chomsky Wolfgang B. Sperlich	Simone de Beauvoir Ursula Tidd
Jorge Luis Borges Jason Wilson	Edgar Allan Poe Kevin Hayes
Erik Satie Mary E. Davis	Gertrude Stein Lucy Daniel

Pablo Neruda

Dominic Moran

REAKTION BOOKS

For Katherine, at last

Published by Reaktion Books Ltd
33 Great Sutton Street
London EC1V ODX, UK
www.reaktionbooks.co.uk

First published 2009

Printed and bound in Great Britain
by CPI Antony Rowe, Chippenham, Wiltshire

British Library Cataloguing in Publication Data
Moran, Dominic (Dominic P.)
    Pablo Neruda. – (Critical lives)
    1. Neruda, Pablo, 1904–1973.
    2. Poets, Chilean – 20th century – Biography.
    I. Title II. Series
    861.6'2-DC22

ISBN: 978 1 86189 514 1

Contents

Neruda during his time as Chilean Ambassador to France, 1971.

Introduction

That most obdurately bookish of writers, Jorge Luis Borges (1899–1986), once reflected, 'Few things have ever happened to me, though I have read a great many.'[1] Nothing could be further from the truth in the case of Pablo Neruda (1904–1973), who led something like the archetypal Latin American literary life, one that often teetered perilously between high drama and the lowest farce, and in which the personal and the public, aesthetics and politics, man and work, were and remain all but inextricable. Perhaps the only writer in the modern age with whom he can be fruitfully compared is Victor Hugo. Besides being a praeternaturally gifted and staggeringly prolific poet, producing more than thirty books of verse which weigh in at over four thousand pages, from an early age he became embroiled in both national and international affairs in ways that were by turns naive, enterprising, courageous, frivolous and often profoundly controversial. In the late 1920s he found himself out in the Far East, witnessing, from out of a miasma of fever, opium fumes and cheap whisky, the death throes of the British Empire. Less than a decade later he was in Spain at the outbreak of the Civil War, an event that turned his world upside down and eventually led him to embrace an increasingly militant communism. In the 1940s, as a fully fledged Party member, he served in the Chilean senate, where his brave protests against a corrupt and oppressive government led him to be stripped of his post and forced into hiding with a price on his head. In the 1950s

and '60s his unbending public adherence to the radical Left
frequently landed him in hot water, especially after persistent
rumours concerning heinous goings-on in the Soviet Union were
confirmed and the USSR took to invading 'insubordinate' Eastern
bloc states at will. In his final years, despite severe ill health, he
campaigned to bring socialism to his native Chile, but lived just
long enough to see General Augusto Pinochet shatter the dream
for which he had fought so tenaciously. Somehow, throughout
all of this, his pen seemed never to rest. These, as the reader will
quickly gather, are no more than heavily edited highlights from a
life bursting with the type of incident and upheaval that would
look more at home in a Romantic melodrama or Mexican soap
opera than in a synoptic and purportedly sane literary biography.
It is, I think, hardly coincidental that Neruda has appeared as
a character in a plethora of novels, plays and stories, as well, of
course, as in Michael Radford's wonderful (though, from a strictly
biographical point of view, wildly inaccurate) film *Il Postino* (1994),
itself based loosely on Antonio Skármeta's novel *Ardiente paciencia*
('Burning Patience'; 1985). As I write this foreword he is about to
be reincarnated by Plácido Domingo in Mexican composer Daniel
Catán's operatic re-imagining of the film, due to be premiered in
Los Angeles in 2009. Perhaps the outsize, gloriously improbable
world of opera will prove to be the one in which the larger-than-life
figure of Neruda finds itself most at home.

It is hardly surprising that a life so crammed with hyperbole
of every sort has elicited extreme, often politically motivated
reactions from critics and biographers, some of whom, such as
fellow hardliner Volodia Teitelboim, veer towards hagiography,
whilst others, like David Schidlowsky, seem bent on performing a
full-scale hatchet job. Certainly it is difficult, perhaps even inappro-
priate, to remain completely impartial when dealing with a life as
flagrantly partisan as Neruda's, and throughout the course of my
own retelling I have no qualms about making my views on certain

matters – Neruda's treatment of the various women in his life, the quality and value of his politically committed poetry, his equivocal, sometimes downright dishonest behaviour in the wake of revelations about Stalin's crimes – abundantly clear. Still, some sort of balance, however precarious, must be struck, and in Neruda's case that necessarily entails acknowledging the dubious juggling acts, feline evasions and often galling inconsistencies that peppered the life of a man who at the same time wrote what is indisputably some of the finest and most original poetry in the Spanish language, and who was constantly willing to rethink, compromise and even sideline his artistic vocation in order to champion popular causes, however dubious some of these may have been. Even fellow Nobel laureate Octavio Paz, who abhorred Neruda's politics, was willing to concede his pre-eminence as a poet, and legions of others, whatever their political allegiances, have hailed him as the greatest writer in any genre ever to have come out of Latin America.

Wherever we look, then, whether in the life or the work, we find a bewildering mass of contradictions: acts of unexampled public valour are undercut by the vilest cowardice in his private affairs; extreme generosity and the most appalling selfishness follow each other without apparent concern or even awareness on the poet's part; embarrassing childishness suddenly gives way to sobriety, common sense and a surprising capacity for pragmatism; earnest advocacy of modesty and parsimony in the lives of proletarian workers is made even as lobster claws are being cracked and champagne corks can be heard popping; exquisite love lyrics, sumptuous nature poems and the most haunting meditations on human transience rub shoulders with the ugliest personal invective and facile, plodding, political rant. A handful of examples should suffice. The same man who heroically sailed halfway round the world to rescue refugees fleeing Franco's Spain was later involved in a B-movie-style gondola chase; while being hunted down by Chile's secret police, he would hold fancy dress parties and make elaborate and insanely risky arrangements for the ingredients of his favourite dishes to be brought to the various safe houses in which he stayed so that he could dine in his customary style; in a dramatic letter in which he announced to his lover in war-torn Spain that he had left his wife, he took time out to ask her to buy him 'as a matter of urgency' a model boat that had taken his fancy.[2] And so it goes on.

Borges once observed of Spanish Golden Age poet Francisco de Quevedo (1580–1645), another indefatigable experimenter with forms, styles and genres, who also did a mean line in political satire and whose own life was awash with conflict and strife, '[He was] not so much a man as a vast, complex literature.'[3] What is true of the Spaniard applies *a fortiori* to Neruda, whose sprawling, dizzyingly varied *oeuvre* hardly seems to be the work of a single poet and defies every attempt at watertight summary or over-arching theorization. Moreover, so intimately are his frequent and often radical changes in subject matter and style linked to specific events and circumstances in his life that to 'thematize' Neruda, that is, to divide his work up, however provisionally, according to a series of discreet aesthetic or philosophical concerns that override basic chronology, is fatally to distort him. None of these intricacies constitute particularly good news for someone facing the task of writing a modest literary biography of a man to whom the very notion of modesty was anathema. Consequently, rather than providing a miniaturized synthesis of existing bio-graphical works, my approach has been to offer the reader enough basic background information for him or her to follow Neruda's labyrinthine wanderings, but to concentrate in as much detail as possible on the poetry that he wrote at critical junctures or tran-sitional moments in his life. Besides citing and commenting on extracts from key poems, in both text and notes I also allude to a wide variety of others, so that the interested reader can consult them and make the relevant comparisons.

Still, having made this fundamental point – that most of Neruda's poetry is autobiographical in ways that make a mockery of modish theories of the 'death of the author' – it remains the case that while his remarkable life is over, the verse lives on independently, and it does so in a world unimaginably different from the one that he believed he was helping to forge half a century or more ago. The question of how much we need or ought to know about a poet's life in order to appreciate his work is, to say the least, a vexed one, and here too Neruda constitutes a complex and contradictory case. He seems to have grasped what is essentially a paradox inherent in the idea of autobiographical poetry (that when writing the most intensely personal verse one must nevertheless do so for a readership which potentially knows nothing of its author) from an early stage. We know from surviving drafts that he excised the most obvious biographical references from his first books, and although in one letter, sent from Ceylon in 1929, we find him boasting to Argentine writer and critic Héctor Eandi, 'Every one of my phrases is impregnated with *me*, they ooze *me*', in another, to Chilean novelist and short story writer José Santos González Vera, he qualifies this claim, saying, with regard to the same verse, 'You'll soon see how I manage to keep an equal distance from abstraction and lived experience, and what a finely honed language I use in order to do so.'[4] Few readers are aware of just how much biographical detail is recorded in the notoriously obscure poetry written in the Far East, and this is precisely because Neruda took great pains to disguise or transform it, to render it at least partially 'abstract' so that the poems must be understood primarily on their own terms. Years later, however, when he had cut his political teeth, he frequently used his poetry to address specific personal or socio-historical issues, including current affairs, and sought to create an unpolished, colloquial poetic voice that was both transparent and sincere. The general readerly response to this aesthetic overhaul may not have been entirely to his liking.

For many, the oblique confessions of the early poetry, despite containing much that is impenetrable, remain more suggestive and intriguing than the unadorned pronouncements of the later verse. Conversely, so localized and limited is the range of reference in many of Neruda's most avowedly 'straightforward' poems, that they have been rendered increasingly enigmatic by the passage of time, at least to the uninformed reader. Worse still, if we avail ourselves of the pertinent contextual sources, the enigmas often quickly reveal themselves as incidentals, even banalities. Of course, this is not always the case, and in his finest political verse Neruda manages to transmute particular personal and collective experiences into compelling and enduring works of art, as anyone who has read 'Explico algunas cosas' ('Let Me Make a Few Things Clear') or 'Canto sobre algunas ruinas' ('Song on Some Ruins'), both written while the first fires of the Spanish Civil War were still blazing, will testify.[5]

In sum, then, we do best to treat both the poems and the experiences that inspired them on a case-by-case basis and, to borrow Isaiah Berlin's terminology, to approach the work as a whole as foxes rather than hedgehogs, remaining sensitive to quirks, discontinuities and thematic and stylistic shifts rather than attempting to bulldoze our way towards some spurious 'fundamental unity' that so many critics have doggedly insisted must underpin one of the most diverse and delightful but also one of the most infuriating and at times dispiriting bodies of poetry produced in modern times.[6] Neruda's work may be uneven, but unevenness can be a virtue. As fellow poet Nicanor Parra once said in his illustrious compatriot's defence, what 'work' is there more uneven than the Andes, and yet who would argue that their protean cragginess does not enhance their elemental allure?[7] This last, homespun analogy reminds us of perhaps the single most startling fact in this most extraordinary of literary lives: this colossus of twentieth-century letters was not born and raised in some vibrant, cosmopolitan metropolis, but in a tiny, rustic backwater, tucked away between the world's longest mountain range and the icy Antarctic waves, at the tip of South America's most isolated country. And yet – cautions and caveats aside – if there is something like an essence or core to this most mercurial of poets, it is in those humble and utterly inauspicious origins that it lies.

1

From the Frontier to the Metropolis

Anyone searching for a common thread amidst the vast and
astonishingly variegated tangle of Neruda's verse should seek it in
the remote southern Chile of his childhood. He was born Ricardo
Eliecer Neftalí Reyes Basoalto on 12 July 1904 in Parral, in the
central wine-growing area of Chile, but two years later his father,
railway worker José del Carmen Reyes Morales, resettled the family
in the more southerly Temuco, now a busy if somewhat drab city
of more than 250,000 inhabitants. Back then, however, it was an
isolated frontier town, so called because it was located on the border
between civilized Chile and the barely charted, often lawless region
beyond, a land never tamed by the Spanish conquistadors which
Neruda would describe in his posthumously published memoirs,
Confieso que he vivido ('I Confess that I Have Lived'), as the country's
'Far West'.[1] Encircled by dense forests, Temuco was largely populated by European and North American settlers seeking to make
their fortune in the booming timber industry, and its streets were
often crowded with itinerant Mapuche Indians who had come from
the surrounding countryside to sell their wares. Neruda's family life
was complex. His mother, Rosa Neftalí Basoalto Opazo, died just
two months after giving birth as a result of complications from
tuberculosis, and his domineering, ill-tempered father raised his
son with the help of his second wife, Trinidad Candia Malverde, a
stepmother Neruda grew to love dearly and whom he would refer
to affectionately as his 'mamadre'. It transpired that José del Carmen

had already fathered a child by Trinidad before marrying Rosa: Neruda's half-brother, Rodolfo, was born as far back as 1895 and brought up in distant Coipúe so as to avoid a public scandal. He later had a daughter, Laura, with a woman named Aurelia Tolrá, whom he met while working away in the port of Talcahuano.[2] All ended up living under the same roof, an arrangement that inevitably caused tensions. However Neftalí, a solitary, self-absorbed child, spent little time in the family home, preferring to wander through the majestic, seemingly boundless forests, rummaging through towering mounds of humus in search of beetles and birds' nests, all the time feeling a 'sort of inebriation' that was his first, tantalizing taste of that 'pure wisdom/of one who knows nothing' that he would later identify as poetry.[3] At night he would stay awake listening to the mournful howling of the wind and the endless drumming of the rain, which he later described as 'the first real character in my life', against the leaky zinc roof.[4] The experience of growing up in those far-flung climes made him a 'life-long poet of the wilderness'.[5] If the woods offered one early source of wonder, another was provided by the sea, to which his father introduced the fledgling poet as late as 1920 during a family trip to the tiny port of Bajo Imperial, later renamed Puerto Saavedra, which they reached by river. In a poem composed more than forty years later Neruda described his first, awed encounter with the thundering southern ocean as a sort of existential awakening, a second birth:

Cuando el mar de entonces
se desplomó como una torre herida,
se incorporó encrespado de su furia,
salí de las raíces,
se me agrandó la patria,
se rompió la unidad de la madera:
la cárcel de los bosques
abrió una puerta verde

por donde entró la ola con su trueno
y se extendió mi vida
con un golpe de mar, en el espacio.[6]

When the sea back then
came crashing down like a wounded tower,
rose curling in its rage,
I left behind my roots,
my homeland grew in size,
the unity of wood was shattered:
the forest prison
opened a green door
letting in a thundering wave,
and, struck by the sea,
my life extended into space.

Critics such as Hernán Loyola have linked these twin domains
(the closed, motionless forests of the interior and the heaving,
open ocean) to maternal and paternal impulses in Neruda's work.[7]
Certainly, Neruda later referred to the former as a sort of protective
womb, a 'maternal wood' from which he felt cruelly expelled when
he left Temuco for Santiago, and in poems such as 'Entrada a la
madera' ('Entry into Wood'; 1935) there is an obvious connection
between the elemental materiality of the wood and the idea of
some primordial, maternal fecundity (the phonetically similar
'madre', 'madera' and 'materia' are cognates in Spanish).[8] In the
despairing 'Vals' ('Waltz'), meanwhile, probably penned in Spain
in the mid-1930s, the homesick poet lamented 'No tengo armas de
mar ni de madera,/no vivo en esta casa' ('I have weapons of neither
sea nor wood,/I do not live in this house').[9] However, there are also
plenty of poems in which the sea is described either as Nature's
womb or even, using flagrantly sexual language, as the poet's bride;
besides, we have no need of Freud to make the more fundamental

point that, however far Neruda travelled from his native Chile and however long he stayed away, spiritually he was never far from home.[10] During his time in the Far East (see chapter Two) and later in Spain (chapter Three) the deep south haunted his verse as a paradise lost, and even during the period of his most fanatical political militancy he would turn to his childhood surroundings as a source of succour and inspiration. In his twilight years, when reflecting on the enigma of human rootlessness and finitude, they provided him with a profound, almost telluric sense of belonging. Though possessed of an unrivalled capacity for self-reinvention, the breathtaking geography around Temuco and his passionate attachment to it remained a constant in his work, helping make Neruda one of the greatest nature poets in the Spanish language.

Neftalí grew into a sickly, sombre and taciturn youth, every bit the budding *poète maudit*, as a poetic self-portrait from the 1950s illustrates:

Yo tenía catrorce años
y era orgullosamente oscuro,
delgado, ceñido y fruncido,
funeral y ceremonioso.[11]

I was fourteen years old
and proudly obscure,
scrawny, scowling and diffident,
funereal and ceremonious.

At school he was not an especially gifted student, achieving mediocre grades in most subjects and repeatedly failing maths, though that particular shortcoming was doubtless a badge of honour for an aspiring poet. His lacklustre performance was presumably due to the fact that he was busy scribbling poetry when he should have been looking at the blackboard – one early

Neruda as a
schoolboy in
Temuco, 1911.

composition is dated 'Chemistry class, July 1920'.[12] Indeed, the
publication of his early notebooks as recently as 1996 demonstrated
that he had been writing feverishly from a remarkably young age
(the earliest entry dates from 1915 and by 1919 he was producing at
least one new poem every couple of days).[13] Unsurprisingly, many
of these early poems are highly derivative, naively betraying the
influence of French Romanticism and Symbolism, particularly
the work of Verlaine and Baudelaire (Neruda's favourite poet at the
time), as well as that of Latin American *Modernismo*, the continent-
wide literary movement headed by the Nicaraguan Rubén Darío
(1867–1916), itself heavily indebted to nineteenth-century French

poetry. Fortunately, French was the one subject at which Neftalí excelled. Neruda would later mock the 'childish melancholy' and 'excessively literary sense of suffering' of those early efforts, though formally speaking they are often impressive, displaying a secure and often sophisticated sense of structure and rhythm.[14] By the age of fifteen he was already a remarkably accomplished sonneteer. When Neftalí was not writing he was reading, though rarely anything on the school syllabus. His early forays into the world of literature were typically eclectic, and he devoured everything from Diderot, Verne, Dumas, Hugo, Colombian sensualist José María Vargas Vila, the now all but forgotten Spaniard Felipe Trigo, Gorky, Ibsen and Strindberg. He also had a weakness for sentimental novels, especially Bernardin de Saint-Pierre's phenomenally popular *Paul et Virginie* and Colombian Jorge Isaac's bestseller *María*.[15] Some of his poems also hint at what could only have been a rudimentary acquaintance with Nietzsche and Schopenhauer, who were much in vogue in Latin American literary circles at the time.[16] He almost certainly encountered the latter's thought through his readings of Spanish novelist Pío Baroja, another early passion. He also ploughed his way through a great deal of Russian literature, to which he was introduced by the headmistress of the local girls' school, Lucila Godoy Alcayaga, better known as the poet Gabriela Mistral (1889–1957), who would become the continent's first Nobel laureate in 1945 and whose path Neruda would later cross, though in far less happy circumstances, in Spain some twenty years later (see chapter Four). Aside from the classics of Tolstoy and Dostoyevsky, he took time out to discover lesser-known authors such as Leonidas Andreyev, whose revolutionary character Sashka Yegulev provided him with an early pseudonym. Those early encounters with Russian writers would prove to be an important source of his youthful flirtation with radical politics. As for poetry, two important anthologies were his constant companions. The first, Enrique

Díez-Canedo and Fernando Fortún's *La poesía francesa moderna* (1913), to which he was introduced by his schoolmaster Ernesto Torrealba, offered an unparalleled introduction to nineteenth- and early twentieth-century French poetry, and Neftalí copied various of its poems (by Sully Prudhomme, Baudelaire, Henri de Régnier, Henri Bataille, André Spire and Jean Richepin) into his notebooks; the second, *Selva lírica* (1917), edited by Julio Molina Núñez and Juan Agustín Araya, contained a similarly wide-ranging selection of Chilean verse. Again, we find transcriptions of many of its poems in the notebooks.

From October 1920 Neftalí began to refer to himself as Pablo Neruda. The reason for the change of name is undisputed: by then he was publishing regularly in local newspapers and journals and he was anxious to conceal his identity from his irascible father, who would much rather have seen his son forging a successful career for himself than frittering away his time and energy on something as frivolous as poetry. However, the origins of what was initially no more than a nom de plume (he did not change his name officially until December 1946) are more mysterious. The 'Pablo' may have been borrowed from one of his favourite French poets, such as Verlaine (who, intriguingly, signed his first published poem 'Pablo Verlaine') or Paul Fort, or even from Bernadin de Saint-Pierre's lovelorn hero Paul. Alternatively, he may have taken it from Dante's pair of star-crossed lovers, Paolo and Francesca, since he sometimes cast himself in the role of the tragic Paolo in his early verse, and signed various pieces using the Italian name.[17] Until quite recently, commentators had little reason to doubt Neruda's own account of how he acquired his new surname, according to which he saw the name Jan Neruda 'in a magazine' and, without realizing that he was a fellow writer, simply liked the sound of it. So, at least, his entertaining but often unreliable memoirs have it.[18] In a late interview he was more specific, claiming to have come across a short story by the Czech writer.[19] However, as Adam

Feinstein has pointed out, the Czech Neruda was not translated into Spanish until 1923, a full three years after Neruda adopted the name.[20] This discrepancy may simply have been a consequence of Neruda's notoriously fallible memory, but some critics thought otherwise. Poet Miguel Atreche, for instance, adducing Neruda's lifelong passion for detective fiction as evidence, reckons that he found it in the first Sherlock Holmes novel, *A Study in Scarlet* (translated into Spanish as *Un crimen extraño* in 1908), where there is mention of a concert by the great violinist Wilhelmine Norman Neruda. The Chilean medic Enrique Robertson Álvarez has taken this hypothesis further, claiming that Neruda may have acquired *both* his names from the cover of a musical score for two Spanish dances by *Pablo* Sarasate (formerly Martín Melitón – perhaps significantly, his 'Pablo' was also a pseudonym), which the composer dedicated to Wilhelmine in 1878 (the score was published in Berlin the following year).[21] Could *this* have been the 'magazine' that Neruda saw? Surprisingly, it could. Temuco was flooded with immigrant German families, any number of whom would have owned a piano. It is, therefore, entirely possible that Neftalí laid eyes on a copy of that score in the Chilean hinterland back in the 1910s, though we shall never know for certain. Jason Wilson, meanwhile, who entertains all the above theories without finally plumping for any of them, throws in one of his own for good measure: that wherever Neftalí first saw the name, it caught his eye because of its orthographic resemblance to that of nineteenth-century French poet Gérard de Nerval (1808–1855), itself a pseudonym for Gérard Labrunie. Contemporaries such as Diego Muñoz attest to Neruda's passion for his arch-Romantic forebear, and Wilson speculates that Neruda may have had Nerval's famous sonnet 'El Desdichado' ('The Ill-fated One') in mind when he styled himself as a lonesome widower in poems such as 'Tango del viudo' ('The Widower's Tango'; see chapter Two). Wilson further points out that adopting a pen name was very much à la mode with Chilean poets of the time, citing Pablo de Rokha (1894–1968), Juvencio Valle (1900–1999), Juan Emar (1893–1964), Rosamel del Valle (1901–1963) and, most famously, Gabriela Mistral (borrowed from French poet Frédéric Mistral [1830–1914]) as examples.[22] The ever mischievous Neruda who, by the end of his life, claimed to have no recollection of how he came to adopt the name, would no doubt have been amused by all the intrigue.

An early portrait signed 'Ricardo Reyes' (Temuco, 1920). The following year he would start to call himself Pablo Neruda.

In March 1921 Neruda left Temuco for Santiago, where he had enrolled at the Pedagogical Institute to train as a French teacher. The poem 'El Tren Nocturno' ('The Night Train'), written in 1962, vividly recreates the long journey north and the acute, almost physical sense of deracination he felt upon arrival:

Y cuando
miré hacia atrás
llovía,
se perdía mi infancia.
Entró el tren fragoroso
en Santiago de Chile, capital,
y ya perdí los árboles,
bajaban las valijas
rostros pálidos, y vi por vez primera
las manos del cinismo:
entré en la multitud que ganaba o perdía,
me acosté en una cama que no aprendió a esperarme,
fatigado dormí como la leña,
y cuando desperté
sentí un dolor de lluvia:
algo me separaba de mi sangre
y al salir asustado por la calle
supe, porque sangraba,
que me habían cortado las raíces.[23]

And when
I looked back
it was raining,
my childhood was vanishing.
The train thundered
into Santiago de Chile, the capital,
and already the trees were lost to me,

pale faces
unloaded suitcases, and for the first time I saw
the hands of cynicism:
I joined the mob of winners and losers,
I lay down on a bed which wasn't ready for me,
shattered, I slept like a log,
and when I woke,
I felt a rain-soaked ache:
something was separating me from my blood
and, when I went out frightened into
the street,
I knew, because I was bleeding,
that my roots had been severed.

Adapting to life in Santiago, then a bustling city of some
half a million people, was a daunting prospect for the withdrawn,
tongue-tied adolescent from the outback, though having contacts
must have helped. Back in Temuco, Neruda had acted as local
correspondent for *Claridad*, the journal of the Chilean Students'
Union, establishing links with editors and critics such as Raúl Silva
Castro, Fernando García Oldini, José Santos González Vera, whom
he had met in Temuco, and Juan Gandulfo, one of its founders. Once
in the capital, they introduced him to a twilight world of painters,
poets and other aspiring literati, who would spend night after night
discussing the European avant-garde, reciting their latest compositions and drinking until dawn and beyond. His friend, Tomás Lago,
provides us with a colourful description of the poet at the time:

He was a tall young man, with a pallid, olive-coloured
complexion, skinny, silent, with a fixed stare and eyes made
from dull ceramic; the most striking thing about his angular
face, which was lined from top to bottom by his sharp nose,
were his black, shady eyebrows which were reminiscent of

birds' feathers, the arches of which would flex into two split, vertical stripes – forming a sort of impenetrable sign – in the centre of his forehead.[24]

In many respects Neruda was fortunate to make it out of the bohemian whirl intact, as many of his contemporaries did not. Some, like fellow poet Romeo Murga (1904–1925), fell victim to tuberculosis, which was rife in the city; others, such as Alberto Rojas Jiménez (1900–1934) or Joaquín Cifuentes Sepúlveda (1900–1929) drank or whored themselves into an early grave. Neruda would end up writing poetic epitaphs for both.[25] It was the seriousness and unflagging determination with which he approached his literary vocation that saved him from a similar fate. Much of his creative activity centred around *Claridad*, his prolonged association with which constituted by far his most important formative intellectual experience. The journal, named after Henri Barbusse's *Clarté* (founded in 1919), was both uncompromisingly anarchist and enterprisingly cosmopolitan in outlook. Besides attracting contributions from leading Chilean and other Latin American writers and intellectuals, it also published articles, extracts, stories, poems and selected *bon mots* by an impressive range of writers and thinkers from beyond the continent, such as Pío Baroja, Miguel de Unamuno, Barbusse himself, Ibsen, Anatole France, José Ortega y Gasset, Strindberg, Whitman, Emerson, Tolstoy, Dostoyevsky, Nietzsche, Gorky, Stirner, Malatesta, Wilde, Tzara and Picabia. Between 1921 and 1926 Neruda contributed more than a hundred pieces, several of which were bellicose political tracts expressly designed to *épater le bourgeois*. Some of the latter, such as 'Scouts', in which he angrily inveighs against the Boy Scout movement for turning innocent young men into mindless killing machines happy to sacrifice themselves for the tyrannical values of the fatherland, are almost laughably hyperbolic.[26] Others, however, such as a series of 'Glosas de la ciudad' ('Glosses on City Life'), offer bleak snapshots of the plight of the impoverished and demoralized urban workforce and the ubiquitous evils of capitalism.[27] Some critics have seen in these youthful tirades, as well as in poems such as the brooding 'Maestranzas de noche' ('Armaments Factories at Night'), the seeds of Neruda's later political militancy. However, as Edmundo Olivares has argued, Neruda's intermittent outbursts of anarchism were iconoclastic rather than heartfelt, part of an intellectual pose that was 'more literary than combative'.[28] The testimony of personal acquaintances such as Tomás Lago corroborates this view, as does the simple fact that the vast majority of Neruda's pieces for *Claridad* have little or nothing to do with politics.[29]

Much more interesting in terms of the political path that he eventually chose to follow are the scores of outraged but eloquent and well-informed articles that the journal published from as early as 1921, which denounce the re-emergence of authoritarianism in post-revolutionary Russia and portray Lenin as a contemptible turncoat and petit-bourgeois dictator. One such piece, from mid-1922, describes the country as 'a vast prison house where there is not a breath of freedom' and Soviet workers as 'the lowliest slaves in the world'.[30] Years later, as news of Stalin's purges and labour camps spread, Neruda, despite having read and enthusiastically endorsed this and countless similar pieces, stated time and again that such atrocities were impossible in what he stubbornly insisted was an earthly paradise.

Ultimately, though, it was poetry rather than politics that fired his imagination, and his literary aspirations were given a significant boost when the poem 'La canción de la fiesta' ('Party Song') won the Students' Union Poetry Prize and was published in *Claridad* on 15 October 1921. A hymn to the vigour and optimism of youth, it is underscored by an earthy eroticism wholly in keeping with another of the journal's core precepts, that of free love. Sex was something else Neruda discovered in the metropolis. Although not wholly inexperienced (in his memoirs he recounts an early, fumbling encounter with an older woman on a threshing floor back in Temuco), the more permissive life of the capital dramatically broadened his libidinal horizons and, as accounts of his contemporaries attest, the callow youth from the provinces rapidly became a notorious Don Juan.[31] His spectacular success with the opposite sex is perhaps a trifle surprising, given that in order to cultivate the image of a demonic *fin de siècle* poet he would flounce around the seedier quarters of town, tailed by a growing coterie of admirers, sporting an ancient, cast-off cape that his father had worn to keep warm when working on the railways. He would recall this string of fleeting but passionate encounters in a searingly erotic poem from his final years:

> *Estudiantil amor con mes de octubre,*
> *con cerezos ardiendo en pobres calles*
> *y tranvías trinando en las esquinas*
> *[. . .]*
> *Con Rosa o Lina o Carmen ya desnudas*
> *[. . .]*
>   *Oh ritmo*
> *de la eléctrica cintura,*
> *oh latigazo claro de la esperma*
> *saliendo de su túnel a la especie!*
> *[. . .]*
> *Amores de una vez, rápidos*
> *y sedientos, llave a llave,*
> *y el orgullo de ser compartidos!*[32]

Student love in the month of October,
with cherry trees ablaze in poor streets
and the bells of trams rounding corners.
[. . .]
With Rosa or Lina or Carmen already naked
[. . .]

                    Oh rhythm
of that electric waist,
oh transparent whiplash of sperm
leaving its tunnel for the species!
[. . .]
Fleeting loves, quick
and thirsty, a fitting together of keys,
and the pride at their being shared!

Thus, with a youthful flourish, began a long, energetic and often
scandalous romantic career. In the midst of his political posturing
and amorous exertions, Neruda's first book, *Crepusculario* (1923;
the untranslatable neologism means either a collector or collection
of sunsets), which he managed to publish by selling or pawning most
of his possessions, including his furniture, his beloved cape and
his father's pocket watch, stands out as a decidedly conservative
affair. Indeed, its recherché title (perhaps inspired by Argentine
poet Leopoldo Lugones's (1874–1938) *Lunario sentimental* of 1909),
along with a good number of its poems, smack of the precious,
modernista aesthetic that many poets of his generation were by
then leaving behind. It is an eclectic mix of refashioned poems
from his notebooks supplemented by new pieces composed in
Santiago, loosely divided into five sections. Although little read
now, at the time it was greeted with unalloyed rapture – at least in
Chile – as the work of a major new talent. One of its poems quickly
entered the popular consciousness. 'Farewell', a brash celebration
of sexual freedom, takes as its starting point a blithe young Loth-
ario's decision to abandon his pregnant lover before she condemns
him to a life of domestic drudgery. Crass and crudely executed
though it may be, it is not difficult to see why the swaggeringly
insouciant refrain 'Amo el amor de los marineros/que besan y
se van' ('I love the love of sailors/who kiss and then leave') was
adopted as a rallying cry by the rebellious and predominantly

The main square/Plaza de Armas in the capital, Santiago, *c.* 1920.

male readership of *Claridad*, where it was originally published under the title 'Canción de adiós' ('Farewell Song') in 1922. The poem proved to be something of an albatross for Neruda. Throughout his life he received endless requests to recite it or had to listen politely while others recited it to him. Even after he had entered the world of national politics, government ministers would apparently greet him with a military salute and, instead of discussing urgent business, reel off the first stanza.[33]

Just a year after the welcome but localized success of *Crepusculario*, Neruda, though not yet twenty, published what would become the best-selling book of poetry ever written in Spanish, *Veinte poemas de amor y una canción desesperada* ('Twenty Love Poems and a Song of Despair'). Given its staggering popularity, one might imagine that it was meticulously planned and executed, but in fact nothing could be further from the truth. We now know that, after seeing *Crepusculario* to press, Neruda wanted to follow it as quickly as possible with a book provisionally titled *Doce poemas de amor y una canción desesperada*, just twelve poems, which he described in a letter to the leading contemporary critic Alone (real name Hernán Díaz Arieta) as 'bits and pieces left over from *Crepusculario*' that he was itching to 'be rid of' since he had 'left that sort of thing behind'.[34] His sights were now set far higher, as a result, he later claimed, of a visionary experience:

> In 1923 I had a strange experience. I had returned home to Temuco. It was after midnight. Before going to bed I opened the bedroom windows. The sky dazzled me. The whole firmament was alive, populated with a teeming throng of stars. The night seemed freshly cleansed and the Antarctic stars were fanning out above my head. I became star-drunk, celestially, cosmically enraptured. I ran to my table and wrote, deliriously, as if it were being dictated to me, the first poem of a book which would have many titles and which would end up being called *El hondero entusiasta* ['The Ardent Slingsman'].[35]

El hondero, then, was the book that Neruda *really* wanted to publish after *Crepusculario*, and his correspondence indicates that he had made significant progress with it (he had apparently composed as many as seventy long poems), as well as planning a series of accompanying volumes provisionally titled *La mujer del hondero* ('The Slingsman's Woman'), *La ciudad del hondero* ('The City of the Slingsman') and *La trompeta en el bosque* ('The Trumpet in the Woods').[36] He had become fixated on the idea of producing a vast, epic cycle of interlocking volumes that 'would encompass man, nature and the passions and happenings that unfolded within it', and this totalizing obsession remained with him in one form or another throughout the following years.[37] The curious title is derived from the work's central, quintessentially Romantic conceit: that of the poet, accompanied by a lover who acts variously as guide, accomplice and protectress, hurling his words into the void in a quest to comprehend and commune with the alien cosmos, like David casting his stones at Goliath. However, *El hondero* was only published, in drastically reduced form, some ten years later. Why the delay? According to Neruda, when he showed the poem written as if in a trance to a friend, literary editor Aliro Oyarzún, the latter immediately remarked on its suspicious resemblance to the work of a then much admired Uruguayan poet, Carlos Sabat Ercasty (1887–1982). Neruda decided to send the poem to Sabat Ercasty himself for a verdict. Sabat, while apparently praising it, confirmed Oyarzún's misgivings, and as a consequence Neruda immediately abandoned the entire *Hondero* project, embarked on a radical revision of his style and expression, returned to those minor 'bits and pieces' of which he had been so eager to disburden himself and came up with the *Veinte poemas de amor* instead.[38] Or so the memoirs have it. In fact, Neruda's is a highly selective version of events (it transpires that he already knew Sabat Ercasty's poetry well, having reviewed it in *Claridad,* and was corresponding with the Uruguayan *before* sending him the poem, which he must have known to be slavishly imitative), but it does contain an important core of truth. Whilst in *El hondero* he was obviously straining to create verse that was ecstatic and incantatory, what he actually produced was sprawling, repetitive and oddly jaded. In response to the rebuff from Sabat Ercasty he determined to 'prune [his] rhetorical and aesthetic excesses' so as to create 'briefer, more intense poems'.[39] As a result of this painstaking revision, the *Veinte poemas*, though sharing much common thematic ground with *El hondero*, are far more taut and concentrated, and all the better for it.

Needless to say, the vast majority of readers have no idea of the aesthetic crisis that gave rise to the book, and simply encounter the poetry head on. What, then, has made it into a bible for young – and not so young – lovers throughout the continent and far beyond, whose verses are lovingly recited by Latin Americans of every race and class, including many who cannot read or write? The question is particularly interesting given that, as a consequence of Neruda's meticulous paring, the poetic idiom of the *Veinte poemas* is highly elliptical and frequently obscure. There are various explanations, the most obvious being the frequent flashes of an explicit, sometimes violent eroticism unprecedented in Spanish American poetry. In the *Veinte poemas* the vague, sublimated longings of Neruda's literary predecessors, the *Modernistas*, are replaced by urges that are unambiguously sexual, and idealized feminine figures make way for a real female body. Poem 1 sets the tone:

> *Cuerpo de mujer, blancas colinas, muslos blancos,*
> *te pareces al mundo en tu actitud de entrega.*
> *Mi cuerpo de labriego salvaje te socava*
> *y hace saltar el hijo del fondo de la tierra.*
> [. . .]
> *Pero cae la hora de la venganza, y te amo.*
> *Cuerpo de piel, de musgo, de leche ávida y firme.*
> *Ah los vasos del pecho! Ah los ojos de ausencia!*
> *Ah las rosas del pubis! Ah tu voz lenta y triste!*[40]

> Body of a woman, white hills, white thighs,
> you are like the world in your pose of surrender.
> My rough peasant's body digs in you
> and makes a child spring from the depths of the earth.
> [. . .]
> But the hour of vengeance strikes, and I love you.
> Body of skin, of moss, of avid, firm milk.
> Oh, the goblets of your breasts! Oh your absent eyes!
> Oh, the roses of your pubis! Oh your slow, sad voice!

Poem 13, meanwhile, opens with a barely veiled reference to oral sex:

He ido marcando con cruces de fuego
el atlas blanco de tu cuerpo.
Mi boca era una araña que cruzaba escondiéndose.
En ti, detrás de ti, temerosa, sedienta.[41]

I have been branding the white atlas of your body
with crosses of fire.
My mouth scurried across you: a spider, trying to hide.
In you, behind you, anxious, thirsty.

This sense of desperate, unassuageable but always physical yearning is palpable even in the most intractable passages. Another key factor in the work's appeal is the majestic setting provided by the mountains, forests and desolate, windswept coastline of southern Chile, a world which might have been designed as a retreat for lovesick poets and purveyors of the pathetic fallacy. Interestingly, this indigenous landscape seems to have been refracted through various foreign literary prisms. One of these, mentioned by Tomás Lago, is Nordic literature, especially the work of Knut Hamsun (1859–1952), whose novel *Pan* (1894) was a favourite amongst Neruda's generation.[42] Hamsun, along with writers such as Selma Lagerlof (1858–1940), seems to have provided a compelling artistic template for what aspiring Chilean writers encountered in the raw. Another, more personal source of inspiration was Rabindranath Tagore (1861–1941), a poet much loved by one of Neruda's early girlfriends, Teresa Vázquez (see below). Neruda's early enthusiasm for Tagore, evident in several of the *Veinte poemas*, would later provoke an ugly and very public clash with a number of Chile's other leading poets (see chapter Four). This awesome natural backdrop does not merely provide local colour or nebulous 'atmosphere'; rather, it acts as a vast mirror or screen that reflects, or onto which the poet projects, his feelings, so that it is often impossible to determine where external geography ends and emotional inscape begins. The opening lines of Poem 18 offer a fine example:

Aquí te amo.
En los oscuros pinos se desenreda el viento.
Fosforece la luna sobre las aguas errantes.
Andan días iguales persiguiéndose.

Se desciñe la niebla en danzantes figuras.
Una gaviota de plata se descuelga del ocaso.
A veces una vela. Altas, altas estrellas.

O la cruz negra de un barco.
Solo.
A veces amanezco, y hasta mi alma está húmeda.
Suena, resuena el mar lejano.
Éste es un puerto.
Aquí te amo.[43]

This is where I love you.
Amidst the dark pines the wind unknots itself.
The moon shimmers on the wandering waters.
Days pursue one another, ever the same.

The mist unfurls in dancing figures.

A silvery gull unhooks itself from the sunset.
From time to time, a sail. Stars high, high above.

Or the black cross of a ship.
Alone.
Sometimes I wake and my very soul is wet.

The sea sounds and resounds in the distance.
This is a port.
This is where I love you.

This subtly orchestrated confusion of landscape and sentiment
again stands in marked contrast to the ethereal *paysages d'âme* of
the Symbolists and *Modernistas*, which were often more allegorical
than real, delicate ciphers for the poet's troubled soul. In the *Veinte
poemas*, on the other hand, Neruda conjures up a realm at once
earthy and rarefied; tangibly, sensuously real yet which simultaneously shimmers and echoes with symbolic suggestion. In effect, we
get two poetic worlds for the price of one. The dual nature of the
setting extends to Neruda's at once robust and elusive use of symbolism. Because it is so difficult to separate inner and outer, subject
and object, it is often hard to establish which elements of a poem are
functioning symbolically and precisely what it is that they symbolize.
Broadly speaking, classical symbolism, in which one thing simply
stands for another, is replaced by a generalized deployment of Eliot's
'objective correlative', according to which a specific object or scene
seems uniquely to embody or reflect an emotion or idea that the poet
otherwise could not name or 'locate'.[44] This lends Neruda's symbols
a peculiar concreteness, which would become a defining feature of
his poetry. When asked about this in a late interview he explained:

> I don't believe in symbols. They are material things. For me, the
> sea, fish, birds have a material existence . . . The word 'symbol'
> doesn't really accommodate the way I think . . . When I see a
> dove I call it a dove. Whether or not it is present in that particu-
> lar moment, for me it has a form, it exists both subjectively and
> objectively, but it is never anything more than a dove.[45]

Another, less subtle reason for the collection's enduring popularity is the presence of several more straightforward, indeed

sometimes rather saccharine lyrics which, despite the dubiousness of their sexual politics, have from the first exerted a potent appeal. The classic instance is Poem 15, which begins:

> *Me gustas cuando callas porque estás como ausente,*
> *y me oyes desde lejos, y mi voz no te toca.*
> *Parece que los ojos se te hubieran volado*
> *y parece que un beso te cerrara la boca.*[46]

> I like it when you are silent because it's as if you were
>   somewhere else
> and you hear me from afar, and my voice does not
>   touch you.
> It's as if your eyes had flown away
> and as if a kiss had sealed your lips.

What for die-hard romantics is a disarmingly childlike love song is frequently viewed by less soft-centred types as a protracted male fantasy, in which the female addressee is infantilized and praised for keeping her mouth shut while, in the final stanza, the poet is afforded a frisson by the thought of her dying. It is surely not by chance that in Mario Vargas Llosa's novel *The Feast of the Goat* (2000), of all the love poems in the Spanish language this is the one that the Peruvian novelist has the monstrous sexual predator General Trujillo cooingly recite just before he performs an unspeakable act of violation on a helpless adolescent girl. Still, none of those often angrily expressed objections has dimmed enthusiasm for the poem, to what must be the considerable consternation of the legions of academic gender theorists who have targeted the *Veinte poemas* in recent decades. At first glance Poem 20, Neruda's single best-loved poem, looks like more of the same, but it turns out to be considerably more subtle. Here, rather than blindly indulging in poetic cliché, Neruda begins by

Albertina Rosa Azócar, dedicatee of many of the *Veinte poemas de amor*, including the famous Poem 15.

foregrounding it, a piece of rhetorical legerdemain that lends the poem, which subsequently bristles with literary and amorous commonplaces, an air of greater sincerity:

Puedo escribir los versos más tristes esta noche.

Escribir, por ejemplo: 'La noche está estrellada,
Y tiritan, azules, los astros, a lo lejos'.[47]

Tonight I can write the saddest lines.

Write, for example: 'The night is all alight,
and the blue stars shiver in the distance.'

It is a simple but effective ploy: because we know that *he* knows
that he is reduced to trotting out lachrymose romantic truisms,
we sympathize with his plight. By resignedly citing platitudes,
then, Neruda manages to reinvigorate them. The poem, throughout
which the speaker struggles in vain to come to terms with his loss,
concludes with a dramatic gesture that literally puts an end to
the affair:

Porque en noches como ésta la tuve entre mis brazos,
mi alma no se contenta con haberla perdido.

Aunque éste sea el ultimo dolor que ella me causa,
y éstos los últimos versos que yo le escribo.[48]

Because on nights such as this I held her in my arms,
my soul cannot accept having lost her.

Even though this be the last pain she causes me,
and these the last lines I write for her.

In fact, the *Veinte poemas* do not, as some critics have claimed,
form a single, coherent narrative, though in his last minute re-
jigging of the poems Neruda, who, despite the *Hondero* debacle,
was still intent on producing at least the semblance of a poetic
cycle, clearly wished to create that impression. Explicit references
to the former undertaking in Poem 1 (written after Sabat Ercasty's
crushing reply) and what appears to be a reworked 'Canción
desesperada' seem expressly designed to suggest that the poet's

traumatic journey has come full circle. The closing scene, which depicts the 'luckless slingsman' wandering alone on the deserted seashore, reminds us of the final and most obvious reason for the book's universal appeal: rarely do we love as desperately as we do during adolescence, and rarely are we so happy to be so wretched, since the more disconsolate we feel, the more exalted and ennobled we imagine ourselves to be. Younger readers identify instantly with those emotions, whilst older ones can relive passions rarely again experienced so intensely.

Their curiosity whetted by the book's blistering eroticism, critics began to ask whether it was no more than the product of an ardent young poet's febrile imagination, or whether some flesh-and-blood muse had inspired it. Neruda never gave a definitive answer, but the closest he came was an autobiographical essay from 1962, later incorporated in his memoirs, in which he spoke of two girls, whom he christened 'Marisol' and 'Marisombra':

> Marisol is the love from the enchanted provinces with immense night stars and eyes dark as the rain-soaked sky of Temuco. She appears with all her joyfulness and lively beauty on almost every page, surrounded by the waters of the port and the half moon above the mountains. Marisombra is the student from the capital. Grey beret, the gentlest eyes, the ever-present honeysuckle fragrance of fleeting student love, the physical release of passionate encounters in the city's hideaways.[49]

The former turned out to be a girl called Teresa León Battiens (also known as Teresa Vázquez), to whom Neruda would refer affectionately as 'Terusa'; the latter was Albertina Rosa Azócar, sister of Neruda's close friend, poet Rubén Azócar, whom he met at the Pedagogical Institute in 1921. As his one hundred and four surviving letters to her eloquently attest, Albertina was the *grande passion* of Neruda's early years, and he remained in love with her –

intermittently, at least – throughout his time on consular duty in the Far East (see chapter Two), continuing to pursue her even after he had returned to Chile in 1932 as a married man. However, attempts to link particular poems with one or the other of the two girls, or to identify two separate sub-cycles within the collection, all founder. Careful scrutiny of biographical sources demonstrates not only that there were several other girls on the scene, but also that Neruda would routinely combine and superpose allusions to and memories of different girls in the same poem. The result is an imaginative composite, an essentially literary creation.[50] As with Dante's Beatrice or Petrarch's Laura, the identity of the real-life models is less important than the skill with which the poet has transformed them into poetic figures. Indeed, Neruda himself later made precisely this point, stressing that poetry's greatness lay in its capacity to transcend the circumstances of its composition and endure as a consequence of its purely literary merits.[51]

Bizarre though it may seem in hindsight, when it first appeared *Veinte poemas de amor* was greeted with a mixture of nervous bemusement and chilly sarcasm by the same critics who had heaped praise on *Crepusculario*. It was, they said, both excessively contrived and wilfully obscure. Nevertheless, this hostile reception, to which Neruda published a disgruntled reply, 'Exégesis y soledad' ('Exegesis and Solitude') in *Claridad*, was in many ways the least of his problems.[52] By now it was clear that he was not going to continue with his academic studies, and he was desperately short of money (needless to say, his books earned him nothing), relying on sporadic handouts from a father increasingly reluctant to finance what he saw as the dissolute life of his layabout son. For the young man viewed by his admirers as the most promising poet of his generation, simply surviving was becoming an issue.

Over the next two years Neruda's reputation as a poet grew rapidly, extending throughout the continent. Despite the initial adverse reactions back home, *Veinte poemas de amor* soon became the talk of the Spanish American literary world. Fame, however, did not put food on the table, and Neruda began to come up with increasingly outlandish schemes to earn a crust. One of these, hatched with the aid of Álvaro Hinojosa, a dynamic, entrepreneurial friend from Valparaíso, involved the production of comic postcards with moving parts called *faciógrafos*, which they attempted to peddle on the streets, without the slightest success. Despite his severely straitened circumstances and the lack of any clear plan for the future, his literary output remained prolific. No new collection appeared in 1925, but in 1926 he published three books, including his first and only essay in prose fiction, the slim novella *El habitante y su esperanza* ('The Inhabitant and His Hope'), a tale of jealousy and murder that again takes place in a fictionalized, quasi-mythical southern Chilean setting, which Neruda now names Cantalao. *Anillos* ('Rings'), meanwhile, consists of a series of prose poems, half of which were composed by Neruda, half by Tomás Lago. Most of Neruda's contributions, especially 'Imperial del Sur' ('Imperial in the South'), 'Provincia de la infancia' ('Childhood Province'), 'Primavera de agosto' ('August Spring') and 'Atardecer' ('Eventide'), longingly evoke the world of the *Veinte poemas*. By far the most important of the new works, however, was *Tentativa del hombre infinito* ('Endeavour of the Infinite Man'), for which Neruda professed a lifelong fondness, describing it as 'one of the true nerve centres of my poetry', but which to this day has received scant and unilluminating attention from critics. Dispensing with punctuation altogether, it is, from a purely formal point of view, the most radical book he ever wrote, a response to the extreme aesthetic exigencies of the day (Neruda later jokingly promised to expiate the sins of his excessively cosmopolitan youth by writing a book consisting solely of punctuation marks) as well as a genuine quest to capture verbally 'thought in all its nakedness, the pure workings of the soul'.[53] A sequence of fifteen poems that, like those of *El hondero*

and the *Veinte poemas*, never really gel to form the intended
whole, both thematically and structurally *Tentativa* reads like
a self-consciously avant-garde rehashing of the two earlier
collections. The constant syntactical disjunctions result in
multiple ambiguities, often making the subject and even the
mood of verbs almost impossible to determine, as the following
tangled excerpt illustrates:

> *Oh matorrales crespos adonde el sueño avanza trenes*
> *oh montón de tierra entusiasta donde de pie sollozo*
> *vértebras de la noche agua tan lejos viento intranquilo rompes*
> *también estrellas crucificadas detrás de la montaña*
> *alza su empuje un ala pasa un vuelo oh noche sin llaves*
> *oh noche mía en mi hora en mi hora furiosa y doliente*
> *eso me levantaba como la ola al alga*
> *acoge mi corazón desventurado*
> *cuando rodeas los animales del sueño*
> *crúzalo con tus vastas correas de silencio*
> *está a tus pies esperando una partida*
> *porque lo pones cara a cara a ti misma noche de hélices negras*
> *y que toda fuerza en él sea fecunda*
> *atada al cielo con estrellas de lluvia*
> *procrea tú amárrate a esa proa minerales azules*
> *embarcado en ese viaje nocturno*[54]

Oh dense thickets towards which sleep pushes trains
oh mound of ardent earth where standing I sob
vertebrae of the night water so distant restless wind you break
also stars crucified behind the mountain
a wing lifts its thrust a flight passes oh night without keys
oh night of mine in my hour in my furious agonizing hour
that lifted me up as the swell lifts seaweed
it shelters my hapless heart

when you encircle the animals of sleep
traverse it with your vast tethers of silence
it is at your feet ready to depart
because oh night of black spirals you place it face to face
    with yourself
and may every force within it be fertile
bound to the sky with rainy stars
on with it, procreate, lash yourself to that prow with its blue
    minerals
embarked on that nocturnal journey

Other translations are possible, and the ungendered object pronouns introduce further uncertainties in the English. Compare this convoluted passage to the similarly frenetic but syntactically transparent opening of the *Hondero* poem that Sabat Ercasty's critique caused him to shelve, of which it may be a conscious reworking:

Hago girar mis brazos como dos aspas locas . . .
En la noche toda ella de metales azules.

Hacia donde las piedras no alcanzan y retornan.
Hacia donde los fuegos oscuros se confunden.
Al pie de las murallas que el viento inmenso abraza.
Corriendo hacia la muerte como un grito hacia el eco.

El lejano, hacia donde ya no hay más que la noche
Y la ola del designio, y la cruz del anhelo.
Dan ganas de gemir el mas largo sollozo.
De bruces, frente al muro que azota el viento inmenso.
[. . .]
Aquí, la zona de mi corazón,
Llena de llanto helado, mojada en sangres tibias.
Desde él, siento saltar las piedras que me anuncian.

[. . .]
Todo de sueños vastos caídos gota a gota.

Todo de furias y olas y mareas vencidas.[55]

I make my arms turn like two wild windmill sails . . .
In the midst of the night, the blue, metallic night.
Towards where rocks and stones don't venture, and return.
Towards where the dark fires mingle and fuse.
At the foot of the walls that the immense wind envelops.
Rushing on towards death like a cry towards its echo.

Far away, towards where nothing is left but night
and the wave of intent, and the cross of yearning.
It makes me want to moan, to let out the longest sob.
Prostrate before the wall that's flailed by the immense wind.
[. . .]
Here, in the precincts of my heart, which are
full of frozen weeping, soaked in warm blood.
From within it, I feel the stones which herald me leaping.
[. . .]
Made up of immense dreams that have fallen drop by drop.
Made up of furies and waves and vanquished tides.

The iconoclastic *Tentativa* may have added to his cachet as a poet, but it did nothing to improve his day-to-day situation. Money remained scarce and stable employment was proving impossible to find. The socio-political atmosphere in Chile was also becoming uncomfortable. The country was in severe economic recession, and military coups in 1924 and 1925 finally led to the emergence of strongman General Carlos Ibáñez as president in May, 1927. His four-year dictatorship, during which civil liberties were suspended and political opponents routinely jailed, marked a dark hiatus in one of Latin America's longest and most stable traditions of parliamentary democracy. As someone with well-known anarchist affiliations, Neruda felt especially vulnerable (Ibáñez banned the publication of *Claridad*) and decided that it was time to try his luck elsewhere. That meant, in the long term at least, Europe, and preferably Paris, long since a Mecca for Latin American writers. He reckoned that some sort of minor consular posting might be a good start, and personal connections eventually secured him an interview with the foreign minister, who invited him to choose from a list of vacant posts. Neruda picked one seemingly at random, though perhaps he was attracted by the exotic-sounding name: Rangoon.

2

Residence on Earth

The years between 1927 and 1935 are commonly referred to as
Neruda's *Residencia* period, since during that time he composed
almost all the poems that would eventually make up what many
consider to be his greatest collection, *Residencia en la tierra*
('Residence on Earth'), first published in Chile in 1933 and then,
in a significantly augmented two-volume edition, in Madrid in 1935.
In literary-critical circles there exists something like a standard
explanation of how Neruda came to write this predominantly
dark and sometimes impenetrably difficult book, eloquently
summarized by pioneering Neruda scholar Robert Pring-Mill:

> Most of the poems in *Residencia I* . . . were written during
> [Neruda's] five years in the Far East . . . His years in the East
> constituted . . . a period of virtually total spiritual blackness –
> the blackest of his life. The sense of isolation present in many
> of the poems of his earlier collections grew into an obsessive
> loneliness, under the pressure of two alien cultures. He had
> nothing in common with the British merchants and adminis-
> trators with whom he had to deal professionally . . . and he also
> failed to establish any real contact with indigenous culture . . .
> His poetry turned in upon itself, recording complete disgust
> with existence, an increasingly morbid preoccupation with
> death and with the passage of time, and a progressive dis-
> integration of the world picture.

Neruda mirrored its collapse in a studied disintegration of poetic form. The organizing principle of the resulting poems lies in his emotional response to chaos. Each text becomes a series of indirect approximations to a clear statement, ebbing and flowing as the response to the central theme alters. Images are open-ended, implying more than they state but often leaving their implications either disturbingly vague or indecipherably hermetic. At times, the syntax disintegrates into a web of multiple ambiguities.[1]

This is as accurate a general account as one could wish for. Between 1927 and 1932 Neruda, accompanied on his outward journey by the free-spirited Álvaro Hinojosa, did indeed occupy a series of very minor and wretchedly paid consular posts in Burma, Ceylon (now Sri Lanka) and Indonesia (he was what was termed in Spanish a 'Cónsul de elección', a sort of honorary consul who in reality was little more than a semi-official lackey); he often felt desperately lonely and unhappy there, as much of his surviving correspondence attests, and many *Residencia* poems reflect those feelings in dense, hypnotic and often perplexingly opaque language. Moreover, even though he changed his working title (*Colección nocturna* ['Nocturnal Collection'], subsequently the title of the first poem he composed after leaving Chile) and kept adding new pieces, some of which relate to events or circumstances that he could not possibly have foreseen, Neruda was aware from early on that he was writing a book that would be defined by a certain uniformity of style and tone. Here too his correspondence, especially the remarkable sequence of letters to Argentine writer and critic Héctor Eandi, provides an invaluable source of information. In April 1929 he wrote: '[*Residencia*] is a heap of verses with a tremendous unity of tone, almost ritualistic, full of suffering and mysteries like those of the poets of old. It has great uniformity, like the same thing begun over and over again, endlessly attempted without success.'[2]

However, there is much more to *Residencia* than this. For a start, at least nine of the thirty-three poems in the first volume were written before Neruda left Chile, and some of them, such as 'Serenata' ('Serenade') date back as far as 1925, before he had any idea that he would be going abroad. In many of those early pieces, such as 'Sabor' ('Taste') and 'Caballo de los sueños' ('Dream Horse'), we can already see him forging a poetic language radically different from that of the *Veinte poemas* and even the avant-garde *Tentativa del hombre infinito*. Perhaps the most extreme example of this is the tortuous, truncated simile that launches the book's opening poem, 'Galope muerto' ('Dead Gallop'), first published in 1926:

> *Como cenizas, como mares poblándose,*
> *en la sumergida lentitud, en lo informe,*
> *o como se oyen desde lo alto de los caminos*
> *cruzar las campanadas en cruz,*
> *teniendo ese sonido ya aparte del metal,*
> *confuso, pesando, haciéndose polvo*
> *en el mismo molino de las formas demasiado lejos.*
> *o recordadas o no vistas,*
> *y el perfume de las ciruelas que rodando a tierra*
> *se pudren en el tiempo, infinitamente verdes.*[3]

Like ashes, like seas swarming,
in the sunken slowness, in the unformed,
or like hearing on the highroad
bellstrokes crossing crosswise,
having that sound now sundered from the metal,
confused, bearing down, turning to dust
in the selfsame mill of forms far beyond reach,
either recalled or yet unseen,
and the aroma of plums rolling to earth
which rot in time, infinitely unripe.

Furthermore, while death and decay obviously loom large here, the poem is anything but straightforwardly autobiographical. In fact, it has more to do with Neruda's readings of Schopenhauer and his desire to create a dynamic idiom capable of capturing the ceaseless waxing and waning of living forms memorably described in *The World as Will and Representation* than with any personal feelings of despair.[4] Indeed, years later he would look back on it with pride as his greatest *exercice de style*.[5] If there was an important literary preamble to Neruda's time in the Far East, there was an equally significant postlude. After returning to Chile in 1932 he was offered further, better remunerated diplomatic positions, first in Buenos Aires and later in Madrid (via Barcelona), a posting which he had long craved. In both capitals he met and caroused with numerous fellow writers and artists, his renown as one of the Spanish-speaking world's greatest poets grew rapidly, and he enjoyed an eye-poppingly active love life. In short, he was happy, or at least far happier than he had been at almost any time during the previous five years. And yet, as Pring-Mill rightly observes, it is from that later period that some of the gloomiest of the *Residencia* poems (not least 'Walking Around', which opens with the desolate line 'Sucede que me canso de ser hombre' ['It happens that I am tired of being a man']) date.[6] This is doubtless because by the early 1930s the poetic world that Neruda had been shaping and refining since the mid-1920s was fully formed, so that he could step into and out of it at will, irrespective of his actual state of mind. We should, therefore, be wary about simply 'reading off' the *Residencia* poems against Neruda's life, or at least doing so on the assumption that they reflect it in a faithful, transparent way.

Before detailing the key events of those first, traumatic years abroad, two general points are worth making. The first concerns Neruda's depiction of life in the Orient, which is almost completely devoid of the heady exoticism that had characterized centuries of travellers' tales, novels, poetry and music, and which can still be found in the works of fellow Spanish-American poets such as Octavio Paz, whose *Ladera este* ('Eastern Slope'; 1968) and *El mono gramático* ('The Monkey Grammarian'; 1973) offer a sanitized, sublimated vision of India, which is treated as an abstract space for poetic and philosophical speculation rather than a concrete historical and geographical setting. As he later made clear in his memoirs, Neruda was deeply sceptical about such embellishment and the sort of tinpot mysticism that often accompanied it, which, in retrospect, and viewed through the lens of socialism, he came to see as a 'sub-product of Western restlessness, neurosis, disorientation and opportunism'.[7] What he encountered in Burma and Ceylon were the ravages of colonialism – poverty, disease, death, appalling injustice – exacerbated by what he considered to be a devastatingly oppressive native religion, the crippling effects of which he would later recall in poems such as 'Lejos de aquí' ('Far from Here') from *Canto general* (1950), and both 'Recuerdo el este' ('I Remember the East') and 'Religión en el Este' ('Religion in the East') from his verse autobiography, *Memorial de Isla Negra* (1964).[8] In sum, there are slim pickings for acolytes of Edward Said in *Residencia en la tierra*. The second point relates to Neruda's own conception of his métier and long-term prospects as a poet during his time away. Significantly, while enduring what many critics have seen as his personal *saison en enfer* (Rimbaud was one of Neruda's favourite poets, so the comparison is tempting, if not especially illuminating, not least because the French poet wrote his ground-breaking book *before* setting off on his travels) he never lost sight of one key objective, which he pursued with near obsessive zeal: to be published – and praised – in Spain. Letter after letter sent from the Far East reiterates this burning desire, and twice Neruda posted copies of the *Residencia* poems to Chilean contacts in Spain in the hope that they would find a publisher.[9] While those attempts proved unsuccessful, his perseverance meant that the manuscript eventually ended up in the hands of the great Spanish poet of the so-called

'Generation of 1927', Rafael Alberti, who, with the help of fellow poet Pedro Salinas, managed to get three of the poems published in the March 1930 edition of José Ortega y Gasset's immensely influential journal *Revista de Occidente*, thereby helping to establish Neruda's reputation in the motherland. So then, however much he suffered in the Far East, we should resist the temptation to romanticize either the way in which he transformed that suffering into verse or the *raison d'être* of the poems themselves. Tortured soul he may have been, but he remained, primarily, a craftsman, and, just as he had done with the *Veinte poemas de amor*, he subjected the texts of *Residencia en la tierra* to continual, painstaking revision. Like the earlier love songs, these poems are not spontaneous, anguished outpourings, even if they frequently give that impression. Similarly, we should not assume that misery and isolation led to complete self-absorption; Neruda was an enormously ambitious young man who was consciously, and with unwavering resolve, putting together a book whose publication he hoped, perhaps even expected, would see him fêted as the greatest Hispanic poet of the day. As so often happened, his wish was eventually granted.

On his long trek out to Burma, Neruda crossed paths with several luminaries of the Hispanic literary world. Chief among these were Jorge Luis Borges, whom he saw briefly in Buenos Aires, and the Peruvian poet César Vallejo (1892–1938), whose acquaintance he made in Paris. The meeting with Borges proved jovial enough, though Neruda, always wary of conspicuous intellectualism, later came to view the Argentine's work as excessively mannered and literary, and reviled him for his political views, which he saw as those of an ultra right-wing 'dinosaur'.[10] The gaunt, funereal Vallejo, by then a fervent communist, was a very different proposition. Many critics consider him to be the greater of the two poets, and Neruda himself probably saw Vallejo as his only credible rival, although, if the account in his memoirs is to be believed, Vallejo

greeted Neruda as 'the greatest of all our poets', comparable only
to Rubén Darío.[11] In his public statements, Neruda, who would
eventually embrace the same political cause, invariably gushed
with praise for his 'good comrade', and later dedicated two poems
to him ('Oda a César Vallejo' ['Ode to César Vallejo'], from the first
volume of *Odas elementales* ['Elemental Odes'; 1954] and 'V' from
Estravagario, 1958).[12] Privately, however, sweetness and light were
often in short supply. For instance, after reading José Bergamín's
prologue to the second edition of Vallejo's revolutionary *Trilce*
(1930, first published 1922), in which the Spanish writer judged
Neruda's poetry to be more monotonous and less supple than the
Peruvian's, he fired off a letter from Java to Chilean diplomat
Carlos Morla Lynch in Madrid, angrily pronouncing Vallejo's
work 'dry' and 'frightful', a 'cruel, literary, sterile book', devoid
of the profound emotion that suffused his own verse.[13] Although
Neruda always claimed to be above literary cat-fighting, that
petulant reaction offers an early example of a ruthless, sometimes
ugly ambition and egocentrism that could override personal allegiances and proper aesthetic judgement. Indeed a further, albeit
less bilious instance of this had already occurred during a brief
sojourn in Madrid in July 1927, when he had tried in vain to
persuade Guillermo de Torre, editor of the important literary
journal *La Gaceta Literaria*, to publish what he later referred to
as the 'earliest originals' of the *Residencia* poems, even though
there could only have been a handful of them at the time. Despite
the fact that De Torre later published a highly complimentary
article on *Residencia*, his refusal to do so still had Neruda smarting
as late as 1950, when he spoke dismissively of the Spanish critic's
pitiful inability to understand his work.[14] After those various
encounters Neruda would have no more direct contact with
Hispanic writers and intellectuals for almost the next five years,
a period during which he would pronounce barely a sentence in
his mother tongue. That linguistic isolation shows through in the

many anglicisms in his letters and must have contributed in some measure to the development of the fractured, oblique expression that is a hallmark of *Residencia*.

The first months in Rangoon were grim. Apart from the overwhelming heat and humidity, the rudimentary accommodation (there was no official residence) and a scarcity of money bordering on indigence, Neruda had precious little to do, merely signing documents authorizing the export of tea and paraffin oil to Chile – an event which occurred once every three months. Despite taking every opportunity to travel – to India, Thailand, Vietnam, China and Japan – his letters speak of misery, solitude, lethargy and a burning desire to escape. But then something of life-changing importance happened. The precise details remain unclear, but at some point in 1928 Neruda met an Anglo-Burmese girl whose real name remains a mystery but to whom he always referred as Josie Bliss. She became his secretary and the two embarked upon the most passionate but also the most harrowing love affair of Neruda's life. They openly cohabited (this was Neruda's first experience of living with a woman) to the considerable disgust of Neruda's British associates, who clearly despised him for 'going native'. Later that year Neruda dedicated to Josie perhaps the most exultant, sensuous love poem he ever penned, 'Juntos nosotros' ('The Two of Us Together'), in which he addresses her as his 'bienamada' ('beloved'), a lavishly literary epithet he would not employ again until he began to write poems for the great love of his autumn years, Matilde Urrutia. 'Juntos nosotros', the expansive tone and sumptuous language of which smack of the biblical Song of Songs (the few touches of conscious exoticism we do find in *Residencia* are all reserved for Josie), is notable for being the first love poem in which Neruda portrays the lovers as an harmonious 'We' rather than the perpetually sundered 'You' and 'I' of the *Veinte poemas*, who remain painfully apart in even the most ardent of embraces. Yet all was not well. Josie seems to have been almost pathologically jealous, repeatedly flying into rages that left Neruda fearing for his life. So terrified did he become that in November he fled Rangoon for Calcutta where Hinojosa, with whom he had fallen out, was already based. During the crossing he began to write the famous 'Tango del viudo', a desolate but touching, at times tragicomic poetic chronicle of his affair with a woman to whom he would later refer as his 'pantera birmana' ('Burmese panther'):

Oh Maligna, ya habrás hallado la carta, ya habrás llorado
de furia,
y habrás insultado el recuerdo de mi madre
llamándola perro podrido y madre de perros,
ya habrás bebido sola, solitaria, el té del atardecer
mirando mis viejos zapatos vacíos para siempre,
y ya no podrás recordar mis enfermedades, mis sueños nocturnos,
mis comidas,
sin maldecirme en voz alta como si estuviera allí aún,
quejándome del trópico, de los coolis corringhis,
de las venenosas fiebres que me hicieron tanto daño,
y de los espantosos ingleses que odio todavía.
[. . .]
Daría este viento del mar gigante por tu brusca respiración
oída en largas noches sin mezcla de olvido,
uniéndose a la atmósfera como el látigo a la piel del caballo.
Y por oírte orinar, en la oscuridad, en el fondo de la casa,
como vertiendo una miel delgada, trémula, argentina, obstinada,
cuántas veces entergaría este coro de sombras que poseo
y el ruido de espadas inútiles que hay en mi alma.[15]

Oh Evil One, by now you must have found the letter, by now you
must have wept with rage
and insulted my mother's memory,

calling her a rotten bitch and mother of dogs,
by now you must have drunk alone, all by yourself, your
    twilight tea
looking at my old shoes, now empty forever,
and now you won't be able to recall my illnesses, my night-time
    dreams, my meals,
without cursing me out loud as if I were still there,
complaining about the tropics, about the *corringhis* coolies,
about the poisonous fevers which did me so much harm,
about the frightful Englishmen I still hate.
[. . .]
I would swap this gigantic sea wind for your sharp breathing
heard during long nights without a trace of oblivion,
merging with the atmosphere like the whip with the horse's
    hide.
And to hear you pee, in the darkness, at the back of the house,
as if you were pouring out a fine honey, tremulous, silvery,
    persistent,
how many times over I would surrender this chorus of shadows
    I possess
and the noise of useless swords which can be heard in my heart.

Yet this was not the end of the story. By the time Neruda
escaped, the Chilean Foreign Office had transferred him to
Ceylon, a post he took up in January 1929. There he was pursued
by the raging Josie, who turned up carrying a rolled-up rug, a
bag of rice (she was apparently unsure whether rice was grown
in Ceylon) and a collection of Paul Robeson records, which they
had listened to together in Rangoon. She caused a public disturb-
ance, and the police warned Neruda that she would be deported
if he did not take her in. She begged him to do so, but he could not.
The terrible scene of their parting is heartbreakingly recounted in
his memoirs:

She begged me to walk her to the boat. When it was about to depart and I had to go ashore, she wrenched herself away from her fellow passengers and, kissing me in an outburst of love and grief, she smothered my face in her tears. As if performing some sort of ritual she kissed my arms, my suit and, suddenly, she slipped down to my shoes, before I could do anything to stop her. When she stood up again, the chalk polish from my white shoes was smeared like flour all over her face. I couldn't ask her to abandon her trip, that she accompany me off the ship that was to take her away for ever. My reason prevented me, but at that precise moment my heart acquired a scar that has never healed. That unrestrained grief, those terrible tears rolling down her chalk-stained face, are still fresh in my memory.[16]

Six years later, when Neruda was putting the finishing touches to *Residencia II* in Madrid, he chose to end the book with a poem titled simply 'Josie Bliss', which concludes with a more oblique though no less painful recreation of that appalling scene:

Ahí están, ahí están
los besos arrastrados por el polvo junto a un triste navío,
ahí están las sonrisas desaparecidas, los trajes que una mano
sacude llamando el alba:
parece que la boca de la muerte no quiere morder rostros,
dedos, palabras, ojos:
ahí estan otra vez como grandes peces que completan el cielo
con su azul material vagamente invencible.[17]

There they are, there they are
the kisses dragged through the dust next to a joyless ship,
there are the vanished smiles, the suits which a hand
shakes calling to the dawn:

it seems that the mouth of death does not wish to devour faces,
fingers, words, eyes:
there they are again like great fish that complete the sky
with their vaguely invincible blue matter.

Although she is never named, Josie's ghost haunts many of the
later poems in *Residencia en la tierra*, such as 'Arte poética' ('Ars
Poetica'), 'Ritual de mis piernas' ('Ritual of My Legs'), 'Oda con
un lamento' ('Ode with a Lament') and the redolently titled 'No
hay olvido (sonata)' ('There is No Forgetting (Sonata)'). Perhaps
the most remarkable is 'Melancolía en las familias' ('Melancholy
in Families') of 1935, a poem ostensibly about the misery caused
by his daughter's critical illness, but in which the poet spends most
of his time longingly recalling the now empty dining room of the
house he shared with Josie in Rangoon. Despite the attempted
exorcism, the memory of Josie persisted. She is the unnamed
but omnipresent 'enemy' of the hate-filled 'Las furias y las penas'
('Furies and Sorrows'; 1934, but not published until *Tercera residencia* in 1947) and as late as 1957, when Neruda returned to Burma
with Matilde, he tried to track her down, recording his futile search
in 'Regreso a una ciudad' ('Return to a City') from *Estravagario*,
which also contains the truly desolate poem 'La desdichada'
('The Unhappy One'), in which he imagines the heartbroken Josie
still awaiting his return. Five years later, in *Memorial de Isla Negra*,
he dedicated two of the collection's most beautiful pieces ('Josie
Bliss I + II') to his former lover.[18] No woman, not even Matilde,
ever meant as much to him. Why, then, was their affair so traumatic, and why was Josie so terribly jealous? Hernán Loyola has
come up with an ingenious hypothesis. He notes that the Buddhist
term *Niruddha* is used to refer to the highest state of consciousness
that can be achieved in tantric yoga. Given Josie's apparent super-
stitiousness (she would constantly chant and perform bizarre
propitiatory rituals around Neruda), might she have thought that

becoming the lover of a mysterious stranger who shared that divine name was part of some cosmic design; that she was, in some sense, 'chosen' to be with him, perhaps even to be consumed with him in some sort of mystical *Liebestod*? Might this account for her near murderous obsession with Neruda and her angry suspicion of any contact that he maintained with his homeland? Might it also explain Neruda's choice of the surname 'Bliss' for his knife-wielding Burmese lover? It is an intriguing and suitably histrionic possibility.[19]

Meanwhile, life in Ceylon brought little solace. If anything, he felt even lonelier there than he had in Rangoon, apparently befriending stray dogs in the search for company.[20] The closest and most enduring bond he formed seems to have been with a mongoose, which became his pet.[21] He sought to allay his sorrows

Posing with a local in a photograph taken by his friend Lionel Wendt, Ceylon, 1929.

by consuming industrial quantities of cheap whisky, a practice to which he was by no means averse in the happier times that lay ahead. What it did bring was an important dose of culture, principally in the form of Anglophone modernist writers such as Eliot, Joyce (two sections of whose *Chamber Music* Neruda would translate in 1933), Huxley and Lawrence, whose books, including a first edition of *Lady Chatterley's Lover*, Neruda borrowed from Anglo-Ceylonese photographer and polymath Lionel Wendt, with whom he struck up a friendship. Traces of his intense reading can be found in some of the very few poems he wrote in 1929 and 1930, especially 'Caballero solo' ('Single Gentleman'), an often hilariously jaundiced view of modern sexuality that glosses the famous 'He, a young man carbuncular, arrives' passage from *The Waste Land*, and 'Ritual de mis piernas'.[22] The latter is a Lawrentian reclaiming of the body from the ankylosing clutches of bourgeois society, inspired, it would seem, both by Clifford's emasculating paralysis and by Connie's musings in chapter Seventeen. The influence of Joyce and Eliot may also be discernible in poems such as 'Walking Around' (1933), which paints a grotesque, often nauseating picture of contemporary urban life, though a decade later, in a shameful volte-face, Neruda would violently reject Eliot as the rotten epitome of the self-regarding, inauthentic bourgeois artist. Neruda also read and re-read *À la Recherche du temps perdu* in Ceylon and, encouraged by Wendt, spent hours listening to César Franck's violin sonata, one of several possible sources for composer Vinteuil's 'little phrase' in Proust's novel. Given the seemingly effortless lyricism of his poetry, Neruda was astonishingly unmusical and had no sense of rhythm (he was a hopelessly leaden-footed dancer), but the sonata clearly bewitched him and, he later claimed, left its imprint on the poems he wrote at the time, thereby creating a minefield for critics intent on pinning down such elusive presences.[23]

A further transfer meant that by June 1930 Neruda was on the move again, this time to take over the consulship in Singapore and Indonesia. After a series of comic-book mishaps, he arrived in Batavia (now Jakarta) on the morning of 13 June.[24] If his creative energies had dwindled in Ceylon, here they were sapped still further, and he composed just five poems (two prose poems and three brief lyric pieces) over the next eighteen months or so. If poetry took a back seat, it was in part because Neruda had more pressing matters on his mind. During his stay in the Far East he had grown uncomfortably aware of the disapproval that his bachelor status aroused in diplomatic circles; it simply wasn't the done thing for a young consul not to have a wife. To remedy this, as well, perhaps, as to lay the ghost of Josie to rest, late in 1929 he had resumed correspondence with his former love, Albertina (perhaps his constant reading of Proust brought her to mind), begging her, in a frantic volley of letters (seven between 17 December and mid-January) to join him in Ceylon. In the last of these, a desperate Neruda resorted to emotional blackmail, threatening to marry someone else – anyone else – if Albertina did not do as he asked. She remained unmoved and, disastrously, Neruda made good on his threat. On 6 December 1930 he married Maryka Antonia Hagenaar Vogelzang (whom he referred to as 'Maruca'), a Dutch-Indonesian woman four years his senior. Hers was to be a tragic story. Neruda never loved Maruca, dolefully evidenced by the fact that he did not compose a single love poem for her (of all Neruda's lovers and muses, she remained dubiously unique in this respect); indeed, the only love poems that Neruda *did* write at this time, the terse, self-mocking 'Cantares' ('Sea Shanties') and 'Lamento lento' ('Slow Lament'), are about Albertina.[25] Maruca is mentioned almost *en passant* in the 'Oda a Federico García Lorca' ('Ode to Federico García Lorca'; 1935) and is the implied addressee of the rather sinister 'Maternidad' ('Maternity'; 1934), in which the poet, who was then partying harder than ever, seems to resent her becoming pregnant, since it means that he might have to acquire a modicum of responsibility.[26] Years later, Neruda would recall her with a sort of embarrassed bewilderment in the poem 'Itinerarios' ('Itineraries') from *Estravagario*, where he asks 'Why did I marry in Batavia?', damningly concluding that he must have been a 'complete, arrant fool' to have done so.[27] Neruda's treatment of his first wife was, in a word, despicable. Back in Santiago (and subsequently in Buenos Aires and Madrid) he would regularly leave her at home while he spent entire nights out drinking and merry-making, and he was repeatedly and unrepentantly unfaithful to her. Even after she had given birth to a desperately sick daughter, Malva Marina, in Madrid, the revelry and casual fornicating continued unabated. Neruda finally abandoned Maruca, in predictably cowardly fashion, in 1936. She eventually returned to Holland, where on 6 October 1939, she put Malva Marina into care in the town of Gouda. There she was to die on 2 March 1943, aged just eight. Neruda did not compose a poem to mark her passing, though later he would write a heartfelt elegy for his dog.[28] The whole, sorry tale was dramatized by Chilean playwright Flavia Radrigán in her *Un ser perfectamente ridículo* ('A Perfectly Ridiculous Being'), written to throw a dampener on the centenary celebrations of 2004 (the title is Neruda's own flippant description of his daughter, whose illness left her horribly deformed).[29] Certain of Neruda's friends, such as Diego Muñoz, defended the poet by claiming that Maruca was haughty and antisocial, had no interest in literary and cultural matters and refused to learn Spanish.[30] Her letters to Neruda's family, which overflow with affection and show an increasingly impressive command of the language, suggest otherwise.[31] Neruda's two subsequent wives, Delia del Carril and Matilde, fared better than the wretched Maruca, but, despite the endless protestations of undying love in his verse, he was unable to remain faithful to either, and his treatment of the former, particularly towards the end of their relationship, was marked by a cowardice and dishonesty that apologists have feebly tried to pass off as reticence and confusion. In short, like so many poets, as a lover Neruda was far better on the page than he was in real life.

With his first wife,
Maria Antonia
Hagenaar
('Maruca'), in
Jakarta, 1930.

Shortly after marrying Maruca, Neruda received news that
he must have been expecting for some time. As one of a series
of austerity measures designed to combat the long-term effects of
the Wall Street Crash, the Chilean Foreign Office decided to close a
number of its minor outposts, including the one in Indonesia. And
so in February 1932 the couple boarded a British cargo vessel, the
Forafric, destined for Chile. During the crossing, Neruda wrote
the last and one of the greatest *Residencia I* poems, 'El fantasma
del buque de carga' ('The Phantom of the Cargo Ship'). The precise
identity of the phantom remains unclear, though the spectral figure

is clearly associated with the poet, who had described himself
as 'a complete ghost' in a letter to his friend González Vera and,
even more despairingly, in a long, rambling letter to Eandi, as 'this
completely absent, utterly remote ghost, whose only remaining
relation is nothingness'.[32] Indeed, by now Neruda was in many ways
a haunted man. He had long since been haunted by the memory of
his homeland, to which he was finally returning, himself a spectre
from the past; he was still haunted by the memory of Josie Bliss and
perhaps also of Albertina, whom he would soon have to face again.
Most of all, however, he was haunted by the knowledge that his
marriage to Maruca had been a terrible mistake. In 1942, when
recalling that long voyage home, he would admit as much via an
oblique but unmistakable allusion, likening himself to Coleridge's
Ancient Mariner with the fateful albatross hanging round his neck.[33]
He was relieved to be on his way back to Chile, but he would much
rather have been returning alone.

3

Spain in the Heart

The Nerudas arrived home on 18 April 1932 to find a country torn apart by political turmoil (there were no fewer than six presidents between November 1931 and December 1932) and reeling from the after-effects of the world recession (copper prices and exports plummeted from 1929, and the peso suffered a series of drastic devaluations). They settled in Santiago, where an acute lack of funds meant that they were forced to rent a single room in a down-town guesthouse. Friends helped Neruda find a part-time job in the library of the Foreign Ministry, though that did little to allevi-ate his dire financial situation, which only began to improve a year later, when he was offered a post in the cultural department of the Ministry of Employment. Largely as an exercise in self-promotion, he started giving public recitals, beginning with a session at a packed Posada del Corregidor on 11 May, during which he read out poems from *Residencia* for the first time. This he chose to do wearing an ornate oriental mask that he had brought back from his travels, and his bizarre apparel attracted at least as much bemused atten-tion as his darkling verses, something that doubtless delighted the attention-seeking poet. A further recital at the Teatro Miraflores on 10 November, this time delivered in near darkness from behind an array of huge painted masks, proved equally successful. These eccentric early performances were important precursors to the many public readings that Neruda would later give when he donned the mantle of 'Poet of the People'. When not honing his declamatory skills, he was busy writing love letters to Albertina behind Maruca's back.[1] He also composed an enigmatic new poem for her, which would replace the original Poem 9 in a significantly revised second edition of the *Veinte poemas de amor* that appeared in June, and which Alone at least greeted with the same ironic aloofness that he had shown first time round, though others, such as Roberto Meza Fuentes, a friend and admirer from his *Claridad* years, were more generous.[2] The bizarre opening lines of this new poem contain an elaborately coded allusion to his former love:

> *Ebrio de trementina y largos besos,*
> *estival, el velero de las rosas dirijo,*
> *torcido hacia la muerte del delgado día,*
> *cimentado en el sólido frenesí marino.*[3]

> Drunk on turpentine and lingering kisses,
> in a summer mood, I steer the ship of roses,
> turned towards the death of the dwindling day,
> rooted in the solid marine frenzy.

Trementina rhymes with Albertina, while her second name, Rosa, is embedded in the extravagant metaphor of line two. The poem's core conceit – that of the poet as storm-tossed sailor – also features in the earlier 'Cantares', another piece secretly dedicated to Albertina (see chapter Two), which begins with a still more idiosyncratic periphrasis:

> *La parracial rosa devora*
> *y sube al cima del santo.*[4]

> The parracial rose devours
> and ascends to the cusp of the saint.

The untranslatable 'parracial' is a neologism forged from 'parra' ('vine') and either 'torrencial' or, perhaps more likely, 'glacial', a reference to her cold indifference in response to his pleading with her to marry him. The saint, meanwhile, is a bitterly ironic reference to the poet himself, recently married but emptied of the passion he once enjoyed with his 'devouring rose'. But what new poetry was Neruda writing at this time? Almost none, it seems; it is as if Maruca's suffocating presence had robbed him of what little inspiration he had left. Between April 1932 and August 1933 he completed just four poems, though all are of exceptional quality. At least two, 'El sur del océano' ('The Southern Ocean') and 'Barcarola' ('Barcarolle'), both of which revisit, though in far more sombre mode, the scenario of the *Veinte poemas*, were probably composed during or just after a pair of trips to Temuco in April and May 1933, the latter to see his sick father. The others, 'Sólo la muerte' ('Only Death') and 'Un día sobresale' ('A Day Emerges'), seem to have been written in a brief burst of activity experienced after his return to Santiago. Correspondences in theme, style and language between this latter pair, along with an announcement in the Buenos Aires journal *Poesía* that Neruda was currently working on a new 'long poem', lead Hernán Loyola to speculate that they were intended to form part of a new sequence unrelated to the still unpublished *Residencia*.[5] If so, it was quickly abandoned.

The new year produced a notable upturn in Neruda's fortunes. It began with the publication of a heavily edited version of *El hondero entusiasta*, prefaced by a cautious foreword explaining the delay in the book's appearance and its indebtedness to Sabat Ercasty. It was surprisingly well received by the critics. Inestimably more significant, however, was the appearance in April of a handsome luxury edition of just 100 copies of the first volume of *Residencia en la tierra*. It initially met with the by then customary mixture of bafflement, outrage and vociferous praise from the poet's inner circle and from other, more perceptive critics, such

At one of his beloved fancy dress parties in Santiago after returning from the Far East, 1932. His fellow revellers are, from the left, Tomás Lago; writer and journalist Joaquín Edwards Bello; Maruca; composer and musician Pablo Garrido; Mina Yáñez and her husband, writer Juan Emar.

as Norberto Pinilla, who immediately identified it as 'a future classic of Chilean literature'.[6] Just months later Neruda was offered a new diplomatic posting in Buenos Aires, a prospect that greatly enthused him. He and Maruca eventually departed Santiago on 28 August. Living in the Argentine capital reinvigorated the world-weary poet. He rapidly formed a circle of intellectual and equally bibulous friends, chief among whom were the poet Oliverio Girondo (1891–1967) and his novelist wife Norah Lange (1905–1972, with whom the hapless mooncalf Borges was infatuated for years), Raúl González Tuñón (1905–1974), whom he would soon meet again, though in very different circumstances, in Spain, and the Chilean novelist María Luisa Bombal (1910–1980), who lived with the Nerudas for a time. He also enjoyed a prodigiously active sex life, though not with Maruca. Among his many conquests was Loreto Bombal, María Luisa's sister, for whom he probably wrote 'Oda con un lamento' (predictably, the lament is for his lost love,

Josie Bliss). Neruda also composed two other profoundly disturbing erotic poems in Buenos Aires: 'Agua sexual' ('Sexual Water'), a compendium of past, partially repressed sexual experiences which, as the title suggests, suddenly come flooding back, and the brutal 'Material nupcial' ('Nuptial Material'), one of the most shocking 'love' poems ever written in Spanish:

De pie como un cerezo sin cáscara ni flores,
especial, encendido, con venas y saliva,
y dedos y testículos,
miro una niña de papel y luna,
horizontal, temblando y respirando y blanca,
y sus pezones como dos cifras separadas,
y la rosal reunión de sus piernas en donde
su sexo de pestañas nocturnas parpadea.
[. . .]
La pondré como una espada o un espejo,
y abriré hasta la muerte sus piernas temerosas
y morderé sus orejas y sus venas
y haré que retroceda con los ojos cerrados
en un espeso río de semen verde.[7]

Standing like a cherry tree without bark or flowers,
unique, burning, with veins and saliva,
and fingers and testicles,
I watch a girl made from paper and moonlight
prone, trembling and breathing and white,
and her nipples like two separate ciphers,
and the rosy meeting of her legs where
the nocturnal lashes of her sex flutter.
[. . .]
I shall place her like a sword or a mirror,
and open unto death her frightened legs

and bite her ears and her veins,
and make her retreat with eyes closed
in a river of thick, green semen.

We are a world away here from the *modernista* daydreaming of
Crepusculario and the exalted romanticism of the *Veinte poemas*.

   The event that had the most profound effect on Neruda during
his Buenos Aires days was undoubtedly meeting the great Spanish
poet and dramatist Federico García Lorca (1898–1936), who was in
the city to promote his new play *Bodas de sangre* ('Blood Wedding').
The two were kindred spirits and established an instant and lasting
rapport, the first literary fruits of which came in the form of the
book *Paloma por dentro*, a collection of Neruda's most recent poems
accompanied by extravagant, sometimes macabre pencil illustrations by his new friend (the final sketch depicts the two poets'
severed heads resting on a blood-spattered table, watched over by a
one-eyed sliver of moon).[8] Besides sharing an astonishing lyric gift,
their childlike (though some would say childish) sense of humour
made them inveterate pranksters and practical jokers. Among their
most celebrated exploits was a recital in honour of Rubén Darío,
which took place at the Hotel Plaza on 28 October. This they con-
ducted *al alimón*, taking turns to speak from opposite ends of the
table (the term, taken from bullfighting, describes a contest in which
two toreadors wield a single cape). Between June 1929 and March
1930 Lorca had spent time in a New York just entering the Great
Depression, an overwhelmingly alienating experience not dissimilar to Neruda's in Asia, which resulted in the nightmarish, at times
barely intelligible poems of *Poeta en Nueva York* ('Poet in New York';
composed 1929–30, first published 1940). Neruda almost certainly
read some of these in Buenos Aires, or at least heard Lorca recite
them (they would often read their poetry to one another), and it is
intriguing to speculate how far they may have influenced the later
Residencia poems. The drear, dehumanizing cityscape of poems

such as 'Vuelta de paseo' ('Back from a Walk') or 'Aurora' ('Dawn')
may well be echoed in 'Walking Around', while there are suggestive
similarities between Lorca's exposé of the numbing protocols of
office life in 'New York (oficina y denuncia)' ('New York (Office and
Denunciation)') and the doleful protestations of 'Desespediente'
('Disaction'), even if the latter is firmly grounded in Neruda's

The last of Lorca's macabre illustrations for the collaborative work *Paloma por dentro*
(1934), showing the two poets' severed heads placed on a table.

personal experience: there was a lot more paperwork to handle in Buenos Aires than there had been in Burma and Indonesia, and processing it felt rather too much like hard work.[9] One also notes several striking similarities of expression between the two collections. Whatever the case, the wretchedness exuded by the poetry did not impinge on their daily existence, which consisted for the most part of a series of riotous soirées and fancy-dress parties. Maruca sat most of these out, but she must have attended one or two, for late in 1933 or early in 1934 she discovered that she was pregnant.[10] Shortly afterwards, in April 1934, Neruda was offered the posting he had hankered after for so long, in Barcelona.

Neruda arrived in Barcelona on 5 May 1934, though from the first his sights were set firmly on Madrid, the cosmopolitan capital and cultural hub of the Second Republic, declared in 1931. He made an initial reconnoitring trip as early as 1 June, and was effusively greeted by his new friend Lorca and Carlos Morla Lynch, with whom he had corresponded while in the East. In his splendid diary/memoir, *En España con Federico García Lorca* ('In Spain with Federico García Lorca'), Morla paints a wonderfully vivid picture of his somewhat shambolic compatriot:

> At last, Neruda. I meet him with Federico in the Baviera Bar . . . He is pale – an ashen pallour – with big, narrow eyes, like black crystal almonds, which are always laughing, but in a passive way, without the least happiness. His badly combed hair is black too, his hands grey. Not a jot of elegance. His pockets are stuffed with bits of paper and newspaper articles. What really captivates me is his voice: a slow, monotonous, nostalgic, almost weary voice, but full of suggestion and charm.[11]

The handshakes were barely over when Neruda proceeded to get so hopelessly drunk that he had to spend most of the following day in bed at Morla's house. Forays such as this one soon persuaded

Tulio Maqueira, Chilean Consul General in Barcelona, that Neruda's heart lay elsewhere, so an ancillary post was created for him at the Madrid consulate, where he worked alongside Gabriela Mistral, the tutelary figure from his childhood. Later, in November 1935, he would take her place after she was hastily transferred to Lisbon following the publication, back in Chile, of a private letter in which she expressed a vehement loathing for Spain and all things Spanish.[12] Once settled in the capital, Neruda resumed a life of what if anything was even more intense socializing, this time in the company of the leading Spanish poets of the day, such as Manuel Altolaguirre (1905–1959), Jorge Guillén (1893–1984), Miguel Hernández (1910–1942) – the 'shepherd poet' whom Neruda took under his wing – and Rafael Alberti (1902–1999), who found Neruda accommodation in the so-called 'Casa de las Flores' ('House of the Flowers') in the Argüelles district, which, much to the dismay of the heavily pregnant and increasingly frail Maruca, quickly became the site of their most Dionysian revels. Lorca, needless to say, was a constant, vital presence, which Neruda celebrated in the 'Oda a Federico García Lorca'. Indeed, it was Lorca who had formally introduced Neruda to Madrid's literary coterie, in a speech delivered before a recital at the university on 6 December 1934:

> Prepare to listen to a genuine poet whose senses have been schooled in a world that is not our world and which few people even perceive. A poet closer to death than to philosophy; closer to pain than to intelligence, closer to blood than to ink. A poet full of mysterious voices which fortunately he himself is unable to decipher; a true man who knows that reeds and swallows are more eternal than a statue's solid cheeks.[13]

This splendid description could equally well have applied to his own, increasingly troubled, verse. Interestingly, given the course that Neruda's poetry would eventually take, Lorca also placed particular emphasis on the profoundly American nature of his friend's verse. Their high-jinks continued even after Maruca gave birth to a daughter (Malva Marina was born on 18 August), who was soon diagnosed with hydrocephaly, a life-threatening condition resulting from a build-up of fluid around the brain that left her head grotesquely swollen. Neruda's immediate response was the harrowing 'Enfermedades en mi casa' ('Illnesses in My Home'), though the terrible anguish described there does not seem to have dissuaded him from spending every night out on the town.

At some point in 1934 Neruda met the woman who, nine years later, would become his second wife. The wealthy Argentine Delia del Carril (affectionately known as 'La Hormiga' or 'The Ant', on account of her bustling energy) was, at fifty, a full twenty years his senior, though her dazzling intelligence and youthful demeanour more than compensated for the difference in age, at least initially. Delia had moved to Madrid from Paris where, under the tutelage of painter Fernand Léger, she had undergone a full-blown conversion to communism. By the time she met Pablo she was militant, and many have claimed that she played a decisive role in his own espousal of the communist cause. They seem to have made little if any effort to conceal their affair. Indeed, as Morla Lynch's diary reveals, Delia went as far as 'looking after' the desperately weak Maruca after the latter had given birth so that she could be constantly at her lover's side.[14] Another particularly grim entry reads:

Yesterday I left Pablo Neruda's house in state of moral asphyxiation. I found his wife, Maruca, alone next to the cot where the sick child was lying. A harrowing, tragic scene, like something out of a nightmare . . . Pablo and Delia were at the cinema . . .[15]

Such frightful neglect led a disenchanted Morla to conclude, 'I like what he writes much more than the man himself.'[16] He was by no means alone in forming such a damning view of the poet. When not busy sashaying around Madrid's nightspots with his new love, Neruda took time out to work on his poetry, and that meant completing the second volume of *Residencia en la tierra*. In September 1935 he finally saw his dream of being published in Spain come true, when Cruz y Raya brought out both volumes in a single edition, which was rapturously greeted by his Spanish poet friends. Nevertheless, Neruda's creative life was not without its vicissitudes, and during that same year he became embroiled in two ugly literary skirmishes. The first was fought at long distance with a group of poets led by iconoclast and tireless self-promoter Vicente Huidobro (1893–1948) and the embittered Pablo de Rokha (1894–1968), a lifelong hater of Neruda, who, in a series of insulting articles published in various Chilean newspapers and literary journals between late 1934 and early 1935, accused him of plagiarizing Tagore in Poem 16 of the *Veinte poemas de amor*. The allegation was unfounded, but it did not stop Neruda responding in the form of 'Aquí estoy' ('Here I Am'), a poem so vicious that it had to be circulated privately as a

Neruda flanked by leading figures from Spain's 'Generation of 1927'; from the left: José Bergamín, Rafael Alberti, Luis Cernuda and Manuel Altolaguirre. Madrid, 1935.

series of unsigned copies, lest its relentless stream of vitriol be traced back to the Chilean consul.[17] The second, partially related clash, involved Juan Ramón Jiménez (1881–1958), already something of an elder statesman of Spanish letters and chief advocate of a by then rather démodé *poésie pure* derived from French Parnassianism and Symbolism. Jiménez, whose wife, Zenobia Camprubí, had translated the poem that Neruda was accused of plagiarizing, had refused to sign an open letter in which various Spanish poets defended their Chilean friend against the charge. The latter initially responded via a series of insulting, anonymous late-night phone calls to Jiménez and later, somewhat less childishly, in the pages of the magazine *Caballo verde para la poesía* ('Green Horse for Poetry'), founded and edited by Neruda himself, who supplied a series of forewords that took the form of thinly veiled attacks on the older poet – the first was pointedly titled 'Sobre una poesía sin pureza' ('On a Poetry without Purity'). The spat, which became increasingly personal (Jiménez later paid Neruda the distinctly back-handed compliment of calling him a 'gran mal poeta' ('great bad poet'), the chaotic product of an unruly continent) dragged on for several years until the two reached an uneasy truce in 1942. Such conflicts were to plague Neruda for the rest of his life, and his response, examples of which we have already seen, was invariably the same: a public declaration of unconcern accompanied by private displays of extreme, sometimes cruel rancour.[18] It is no wonder that Delia, despite indulging his every whim, often described him as a big baby.[19]

The sheer pettiness of such clashes is embarrassingly magnified if we shift our gaze to the contemporary political scene. Madrid in the early 1930s may have been a paradise for artists and intellectuals, but the country as a whole was fatally polarized by a long-standing rift between Right (represented by the old land-owning classes, the Catholic Church and large sections of the military) and Left (weakened by internal divisions between moderate Republicans, socialists and anarchists), which eventually resulted in the outbreak of the Spanish Civil War on 18 July 1936. A month later, Lorca was dead, murdered by Franco's henchmen. Neruda's reaction came in the form of his first book of committed poetry, *España en el corazón* ('Spain in Our Hearts'; 1937), at once an impassioned tirade against the invading Nationalist forces and a hymn to the Republic and its defenders. At its heart lies the explosive 'Explico algunas coas', in which he publicly accounts for his sudden change of tack. It opens with a dramatic renunciation of the morbid navel-gazing of *Residencia*:

> *Preguntaréis: Y dónde están las lilas?*
> *Y la metafísica cubierta de amapolas?*
> *Y la lluvia que a menudo golpeaba*
> *sus palabras llenándolas*
> *de agujeros y pájaros?*

> *Os voy a contar todo lo que me pasa.*[20]

> You're bound to ask: And where are the lilacs?
> And the metaphysics laden with poppies?
> And the rain which often battered
> his words filling them
> with holes and birds?

> I'm going to tell you everything that's happening to me.

The first line, which plunges the reader into an urgent dialogue with the poet, is a conscious, combative reprise of the much more tentative opening of 'No hay olvido (sonata)', penned shortly before, which begins 'Si me preguntáis en dónde he estado/debo decir "Sucede"' ('If you ask me where I've been/I can only say "Things happen"').[21] Neruda then goes on to paint a deliberately idealized picture of Spain prior to Franco's uprising, appealing to his friends, including the dead Lorca, to confirm the veracity of his account. Suddenly the idyll is engulfed by a wave of gunfire, flames and blood:

Y una mañana todo estaba ardiendo
y una mañana las hogueras
salían de la tierra
devorando seres
[. . .]
Bandidos con frailes negros bendiciendo
venían por el cielo a matar niños,
y por la calle la sangre de los niños
corría simplemente, como sangre de niños.[22]

And then one morning everything was ablaze
and then one morning bonfires
came out of the earth
devouring everything alive.
[. . .]
Bandits with black friars giving their blessing
came through the air to kill children,
and through the streets the blood of children
flowed simply, like children's blood.

Note the poet's refusal to embellish that last, devastating simile with a comparative term that might distract us from its awful immediacy – it would be shameful to 'poeticize' such horrors. The poem ends by coming full circle, re-posing the initial question and firing back a resounding, thrice-repeated answer:

Venid a ver la sangre por las calles,
venid a ver
la sangre por las calles,

venid a ver la sangre
por las calles![23]

Come and see the blood in the streets,
Come and see
The blood in the streets,
Come and see the blood
In the streets!

Whereas some poems in *España en el corazón* are little more than rhyming propaganda, crude invective or noisy calls to arms, 'Explico algunas cosas' is so compelling because it convincingly dramatizes Neruda's relinquishing of his former, self-absorbed aesthetic when faced with the collective horror that now surrounded him. How could he *not* write about it? Much of his later political verse is tainted by what Robert Pring-Mill correctly identifies as a tendency to 'degenerate into raucous diatribe', often fuelled by a woeful ideological blinkeredness, but there is no such vapid tub-thumping here, just properly defiant indignation.[24] There has been much critical debate regarding the precise nature of Neruda's political *prise de conscience*. As I indicated in chapter One, it is unlikely to have resulted from a resurgence of his largely cosmetic youthful anarchism. Besides, as events around him unfolded Neruda became ever more contemptuous of the anarchists' recklessness and acts of wanton cruelty.[25] Some, like Amado Alonso, see it as a sudden, almost Pauline conversion.[26] Certainly, in 1933, in another letter to Eandi, we find him pouring scorn on proletarian art and declaring his independence as a politically unaffiliated 'romantic intellectual' who prefers 'dreams' to 'Moscow, armoured trains, etc.', while as recently as January 1935, in a letter to Miguel Hernández, he had praised the latter's 'goats and nightingales' over the dour efforts of 'communist poets', whom he evidently loathed.[27] Others view it as the culmination of a more gradual process, citing the influence of

Delia del Carril and perfervid Communist poets such as Alberti
(who had made his first pilgrimage to Moscow in 1932 and would
return in 1933, 1934 and 1937, at the height of the terror, to take tea
with Stalin), the newly converted Hernández, who would follow suit
in 1937 and who later dedicated his book *El hombre acecha* ('Man
Lies in Wait'; 1939) to Neruda, and González Tuñón, both of whom
are addressed in 'Explico algunas cosas', as determining factors.
Loyola pinpoints the publication of 'Tres cantos materiales' ('Three
Material Songs'; 1935) as a key moment (the title hints at a material-
ism with possible Marxist overtones) as well as seeing in some of
the later *Residencia* poems, such as 'Estatuto del vino' ('Statute of
Wine'), 'Apogeo del apio' ('Apogee of Celery'), 'El desenterrado'
('The Unburied One'), 'La calle destruida' ('The Destroyed Street')
and 'Vuelve el otoño' ('Autumn Returns'), covert allusions to the
brutal repression of a miners' strike in Asturias in 1934, clinically
orchestrated by none other than General Francisco Franco. Gerald
Brenan described the latter as the 'first battle of the Spanish Civil
War', and it is the subject of González Tuñón's outraged collection
La rosa blindada ('The Armour-plated Rose'; 1935), which Neruda
certainly read, and in which Delia is the dedicatee of one of the
poems, 'El Arco de la Sangre' ('The Arch of Blood').[28] Nevertheless,
aside from a fleeting acknowledgement in the poem 'El amor' ('Love';
1943), publicly at least Neruda gave Delia scant credit for his conversion to socialism, and Alberti reported that Neruda expressed
no real interest in organized politics prior to the Civil War.[29] The
decisive factor was probably the death of Lorca, in which the political
and the personal painfully converged. Lorca had long since professed socialist sympathies, and it is in the 'Oda a Federico García
Lorca' that Neruda's most explicit socio-political references can be
found prior to the publication of *España en el corazón*. As Loyola
points out, Neruda's poetry, including his political verse, almost
always required some sort of catalyst in lived experience, and none
was more powerful than Lorca's friendship.[30] His initial sympathy

Neruda's diplomatic visa in Spain, dated 4 January, 1936. He appears as Ricardo Reyes and his original, makeshift job title of 'Attaché to the Chilean Embassy' has been changed to 'Chilean Consul', seemingly in his own hand.

for the Republican cause was, then, more visceral than ideological, underpinned by a basic humanitarianism rather than by any coherent political programme. Indeed, in his official correspondence at the time he states categorically that he was an anti-fascist, not a communist (he would not join the Communist Party officially until 1945).[31] This 'intuitive' approach to politics persisted throughout Neruda's life, and often landed him in trouble as a consequence of his inability or refusal to distinguish between the abstract notion of comradely solidarity and the tyrannical political systems often imposed in its name, between high ideals and ugly *Realpolitik*.

One final, less obviously political factor also seems to have contributed to the change of tone in Neruda's poetry in the mid-1930s. In a speech delivered in 1942, he revealed how his constant reading of Quevedo's poetry eventually cured him of his obsession with death, which he came to see as an immanent, constitutive part of a life that was greater than the sum of its perishable, finite parts. Crucially, he insisted that this metaphysical revelation was inseparable from his discovery of Spain and his experiences during the Spanish Civil War.[32]

Neruda now devoted all his energy to aiding the Republic, often clashing with the Chilean Foreign Ministry back home for breaching diplomatic neutrality (his increasingly partisan interventions eventually cost him his post, and there was no offer of a new placement). Reading his own account of those first, traumatic months following the outbreak of the war, as well as those of his leading biographers, one forms a picture of a fearless freedom fighter willing to risk life and limb for the sake of the cause. However, as Morla Lynch's recently published diaries suggest, his career as a Republican activist had a less than heroic start. The entry for 11 November 1936 describes a 'terrified Pablo Neruda [who], thinking only of himself, closes the Consulate'.[33] He was evidently in a hurry, for on that same day he left Madrid first for Valencia, then Barcelona, and finally Marseilles, where he took leave of Maruca and Malva Marina, who were making their escape to Holland. He would never see them again. In a letter from the French port, dated 10 December, he informed Delia that he had broken definitively from the wife whom he had long despised, and begged her to join him.[34] He then decamped to Paris where, after a joyous reunion with Delia, who had heeded his call, he threw himself headlong into politics, undertaking various projects designed to whip up pro-Republican support from the sanctuary of the French capital. These included the creation of the journal *Los poetas del mundo defienden el pueblo español* (The Poets of the World Defend the Spanish People), in which he was accompanied by Nancy Cunard (great-granddaughter of the famous shipping magnate), and in the fifth number of which Auden's controversial poem 'Spain' appeared. Delia introduced him to leading Communist writers and intellectuals, chief among whom were Paul Éluard (1895–1952) and Cunard's former lover, Louis Aragon (1897–1982). With the help of Delia and González Tuñón, amongst others, he set about organizing the Latin American delegation to the Second International Congress of Writers for the Defence of Culture (the first had taken place in Paris in 1935), which, in a gesture of solidarity with the besieged Spanish Republic, took place in Valencia and Madrid on 4, 6 and 7 July 1937, before moving on to Barcelona (11 July) and finally Paris, where the closing session took place on 17 July. This huge event proved to be spectacularly ineffectual, unless one counts a few vague and hastily formulated promises to raise global consciousness of Spain's plight as significant progress. Instead, it was dominated by the sort of petty squabbling and futile ideological wrangling at which egomaniacal artists and writers excel. The Stalinists quickly imposed themselves, and they needed to, as there was plenty of reparatory propaganda work to be done. Just a month after the outbreak of the Civil War, the first of a series of farcical show trials (the infamous Zinoviev/Kamenev trial) had taken place in Moscow, with a second (the so-called 'Trial of the Seventeen') following in January 1937, and only weeks before the Congress Andreu Nin, leader of the breakaway POUM (Workers' Party of Marxist Unification), had been arrested, tortured and butchered (rumour has it that he was flayed alive) on Stalin's orders. Throughout the cafés and bars of Valencia, grave doubt was already being cast on the garishly theatrical cover story: that Nin was a Trotskyite in the pay of Hitler and had been rescued by a group of fellow Nazis and spirited away either to Franco's centre of operations in Burgos or to Berlin. Neruda was present at many such discussions, but for the sake of solidarity thought it expedient to remain silent. There would be many more occasions on which his allegiance to the Party would lead him to follow the same course. The Soviet hard-liners, along with Spanish luminaries such as José Bergamín, also spent much time berating André Gide, whose prescient *Retour de l'URSS* (*Return from the USSR*; 1936) had painted a less than flattering picture of life in the Soviet 'utopia'. As Neruda's own position became increasingly radical, he would add his voice to theirs, scorning Gide (amongst others) in 'Los poetas celestes' ('The Poets with Their Heads in the Clouds'; 1950) for turning their backs on human suffering in their narcissistic search for ideal beauty.[35] It was also at the Valencia conference that Neruda met the young Mexican poet Octavio Paz (1914–1998), though, as we shall see, politics was soon to drive a wedge between them.

Meanwhile, stripped indefinitely of his consular status, and with the situation in Spain looking increasingly hopeless, it was finally time to return to Chile, and he and Delia set sail for Valparaíso on 28 August.

4

A Vision of America

The years between 1937 and 1950 constitute the protracted gestation period of Neruda's most ambitious work, the vast *Canto general* ('General Song'), the twin sources of inspiration for which were an ever firmer if always rather ill-formulated adherence to the Marxist view of history and a growing sense of *Americanismo*: that is, the belief in a common identity and sense of purpose shared by the constituent nations and cultures of Latin America, which it was the poet's task to articulate and promote. Still, all that lay a long way off, and Neruda's first action on returning to Chile was to form the Alliance of Chilean Intellectuals, the principal goal of which was to alert the nation to the growing menace of international Fascism, which Neruda had witnessed at first hand in Spain. As he stressed in an interview with Peruvian journalist and left-wing activist Mariano Seoane in December 1937, in which he again denied being a communist, the Alliance's opposition to Fascism was primarily cultural and ethical, not ideological.[1] A month earlier, Chilean publishing house Ercilla had printed the first complete edition of *España en el corazón*. The first Spanish edition appeared almost exactly a year later, on 7 November 1938, and another was scheduled for publication in January 1939. Neruda tells a remarkable story about the preparation of that second Spanish edition, very few copies of which ever saw the light of day. Apparently, because of a shortage of paper, soldiers working under the supervision of poet Manuel Altolaguirre at a paper mill near the old monastery of

Montserrat, not far from Gerona, used anything they had to hand, including bits of cloth, bandages, an enemy flag and even the uniform of one of Franco's troops, to make the paper.[2] It is a wonderful tale, its only drawback being that it is almost certainly fictitious. Not only is the quality of paper in the surviving copies far too high, no trace of a paper mill in the entire region surrounding the monastery has ever been found. True or not, the book was soon to play a decisive part in Neruda's ongoing political conversion, though in the least expected of ways. Once back in Chile, he had taken to giving public recitals again, and one of these, delivered to members of the Porters' Union in Santiago's central market early in 1938, was to have a life-altering effect on him. Having failed to prepare a speech, he grabbed a copy of *España en el corazón* and ended up reading it out cover to cover. When he had finished, the men, who had remained unnervingly silent throughout, began to sob with emotion. At least that is how Neruda remembered the episode when he recounted it for the first time a full twelve years later.[3] Whatever the case, it was apparently from that moment on that he started to conceive of himself first and foremost as a spokesman whose duty it was to address and represent the downtrodden, disenfranchised *pueblo* as clearly and directly as possible. Over the course of the following years he would commonly portray himself as just one more humble, honest worker among the faceless multitude and describe his poetry as a trade qualitatively and practically no different from those of carpentry, baking or mining. Many other formerly hermetic poets would follow a similar path. His friend Rafael Alberti, for instance, later created an alter ego, Juan Panadero ('Juan Baker') who penned, *inter alia*, ersatz popular verse and panegyrics to Stalin. Neruda also became increasingly scornful of intellectual and academic approaches to his work, as a consequence of which his language and rhetoric became correspondingly prosaic and divided the critics more violently than ever. The following lines from 'La gran alegría' ('Great Happiness'; 1950) sum up his new attitude:

No escribo para que otros libros me aprisionen
ni para encarnizados aprendices de lirio,
sino para sencillos habitantes que piden
agua y luna, elementos del orden inmutable,
escuelas, pan y vino, guitarras y herramientas.

Escribo para el pueblo, aunque no pueda
leer mi poesía con sus ojos rurales.
[. . .]
Quiero que a la salida de las fábricas y minas
esté mi poesía adherida a la tierra,
al aire, a la victoria del hombre maltratado.[4]

I don't write so that other books can ensnare me
nor for crazed trainee Verlaines,
but rather for simple folk who ask for
water and moonlight, staples of the immutable order,
schools, bread and wine, guitars and tools.

I write for the people, even if they cannot
read my poetry with their rustic eyes.
[. . .]
At the gates of factories and mines
I want my poetry to cling to the earth,
to the air, to the victory of abused mankind.

The year 1938 was overshadowed by the loss of both his parents.
His father, with whom he had never enjoyed a comfortable relationship, died on 7 May, followed just months later, on 18 August, by
his beloved stepmother. Early in 1939 Neruda undertook an
important humanitarian mission that he always recalled with
pride. It was now abundantly clear that Franco's Nationalists
would emerge victorious in the Spanish Civil War and this led

to grave concern for the hundreds of thousands of Republican refugees attempting to leave the country. Consequently, at the bidding of newly elected populist president Pedro Aguirre Cerda, Neruda, accompanied by Delia, set off for France with instructions to bring back to Chile as many of the fleeing Spaniards who had made it over the Pyrenees as possible. It was a mammoth and constantly imperilled task, but Neruda eventually secured a boat, the *Winnipeg*, which left Bordeaux for Valparaíso on 4 August 1939, crammed with more than two thousand Spaniards, one of whom would later return Neruda's generous favour in similarly dramatic circumstances.[5] Neruda later described this rescue operation as more important to him than all the poetry he had ever written.[6]

When he and Delia finally returned to Chile in January 1940, an exhausted Neruda decided that he needed a retreat where he could write undisturbed, and bought a simple stone house at Isla Negra, on a secluded stretch of coast just south of Valparaíso. Neruda, who later dubbed himself 'treasurer of the sea', cherished the proximity

A view of Neruda's famously eccentric house at Isla Negra.

to the ocean, and it was at Isla Negra that he penned some of the most beautiful marine poetry in Spanish.[7] The house is now a shrine for tourists, who flock there in their thousands to see Neruda's various collections of exotica, which include tribal masks, ships' figureheads and a vast array of shells. There was little time to settle in, however, for soon afterwards the Foreign Ministry finally offered him a new diplomatic posting, this time as Consul General in Mexico. Mexico filled Neruda with a passion and reverence akin to those experienced by fellow poets such as André Breton and Antonin Artaud, both of whom had recently visited the country, and inspired some of his finest poetry.[8] His enthusiasm is hardly surprising, given the prevailing socio-political climate. Socialist president Lázaro Cárdenas had instituted sweeping agrarian reforms, nationalized major US oil companies and ensured that Mexico welcomed more Spanish refugees – including many leading writers and intellectuals – than any other Latin American country. Moreover, there was a tangible sense in which the country, rebuilding itself in the wake of the Revolution (1910–17), had embarked on a dynamic period of national self-discovery, what Octavio Paz would describe almost mystically as an 'immersion of Mexico in its own being'.[9] This manifested itself in a tremendous burgeoning of the arts, by far the most important manifestation of which were the murals of Diego Rivera (1886–1957), José Clemente Orozco (1883–1949) and David Alfaro Siqueiros (1896–1974). Critics have claimed that these exerted a profound influence on Neruda's ever-broadening conception of the still embryonic *Canto general* (at this stage Neruda intended to write only a *Canto general de Chile*, which would eventually form just a single section in the completed work).[10] It is a compelling argument. The murals were a fundamentally democratic art form, since they adorned public buildings to which everyone had access; they were also painted in a style that was popular, approachable and quintessentially Mexican; finally, and perhaps most importantly, these huge mosaics were able to encompass great chunks of Mexican history simultaneously, juxtaposing key figures and events on a single canvas. It is hardly surprising, then, that Neruda later got Rivera and Siqueiros to provide the illustrations for the first edition of his own literary tapestry. His Mexican experience also helped persuade Neruda that there were common threads in the history and culture of Latin American nations that might fruitfully be entwined. That conviction was soon reinforced as a consequence of what initially were dubious circumstances. Soon after his arrival, without seeking permission from the Foreign Ministry, Neruda issued a visa to Siqueiros, who had been imprisoned for his part in the attempted murder of Trotsky, to whom Cárdenas had granted asylum in 1937 and who was eventually assassinated on 20 August 1940. For many years afterwards, Neruda was denounced by his political detractors as an accomplice, though no hard evidence has ever come to light to support the accusation. Still, if he wanted to avoid such suspicions he kept entirely the wrong sort of company. Many of his closest acquaintances in Mexico were militant Stalinists, one of whom, photographer and political activist Tina Modotti, died in mysterious circumstances in a taxi in Mexico City in 1942, aged just forty-five. Many believed that she was assassinated on the orders of her partner, notorious Stalinist henchman Vittorio Vidali. Vidali, who is also thought to have had a hand in the murder of Modotti's previous partner, the Cuban communist leader Julio Antonio Mella, had also participated in the failed attempt on Trotsky's life, and had been instrumental in introducing his eventual assassin, Ramón Mercader, into Trotsky's inner circle. Under the *nom de guerre* Comandante Carlos Contreras, he had also participated in the kidnapping and horrific slaying of Andreu Nin back in Spain, where he took part in hundreds of Soviet-sanctioned executions of Communist 'dissidents' (to give an idea of just how skewed critical vision had become at the time, Rafael Alberti referred to Vidali as 'a brave and incredibly cultured man, a true lover of intellectuals').[11] Modotti, it seems, knew too much and, besides, she was apparently beginning to harbour doubts about the nobility of the cause. Could Neruda, especially given his recent experiences in Spain, really have remained in the dark about all of this? Whatever the case, these were hardly the circles in which a Chilean consul ought to be moving. The outcome of his aiding Siqueiros was a severe reprimand and a two-month suspension without pay. The enforced break allowed Neruda to travel to Guatemala, then languishing under the brutal dictator-ship of Jorge Ubico. There he met novelist Miguel Ángel Asturias (1899–1974), the future Nobel laureate (1967), whose friendship would later prove vitally important, and gave an incredibly tense public recital during which machine guns were trained on him. That hair-raising experience bolstered his sense of civic duty as a poet as well as his growing realization that Latin American countries faced a series of common, age-old dilemmas, principal among which was political authoritarianism, unsolicited gift of the Spanish Conquistadors.

Back in Mexico, he indulged in one of his favourite extracur-ricular activities – literary mud-slinging – this time with Octavio Paz. Both temperamentally and politically, the two men were poles apart. Neruda was earthy and intuitive, guided predominantly by gut feeling; Paz was cool, reflective, analytical. While Neruda had enthusiastically embraced the popular cause and adapted his poetry accordingly, Paz, ever since witnessing the Stalinist bullying at the Valencia conference and the public vilification of André Gide, had become increasingly suspicious of the Soviet experiment and had no time for committed art, which he viewed as facile propaganda. Their falling out is linked in the main to the publication of the important Panhispanic poetry anthology *Laurel* (1941), of which Paz was one of four co-editors. The book was commissioned by Séneca, a publishing house run by exiled Spanish intellectual José Bergamín. Despite the fact that Bergamín was responsible for publishing the two-volume edition of *Residencia* back in 1935 and enthusiastically shared Neruda's political views, he had fallen from the Chilean's favour for reasons that remain unclear, though, in spite of the Spaniard's subsequent generosity, it is possible that Neruda had never stopped smarting from the negative comments in Bergamín's prologue to Vallejo's *Trilce* back in 1930 (see chapter Two); he certainly had an elephantine memory for insult. In typically puerile fashion, Neruda accused Paz of taking sides by agreeing to collaborate on *Laurel*. He also upbraided him for not including enough socially committed poetry in the volume, especially that of Miguel Hernández, who was then wasting away in a Spanish gaol, where he died of tuberculosis in 1942. Neruda then deliberately waited until the book had gone to press – the most awkward possible moment – before formally requesting that his own contribution be withdrawn. The feud seems to have come to a head at a dinner held in Neruda's honour at the Spanish Republican Centre in Mexico City several weeks after *Laurel* finally appeared, when a desperately inebriated Pablo, in an all too familiar display of pettiness, unleashed a stream of the crudest insults at the 'bourgeois' Paz. According to the latter, the two nearly came to blows and had to be separated by friends.[12] Enough was enough. After publishing 'Respuesta a un cónsul' ('Reply to a Consul'), an excoriating attack on Neruda's personality and his poetry carefully timed to correspond with the latter's departure from Mexico, Paz would not speak to his former friend and mentor for twenty-five years.[13]

Hindsight perhaps confers an unfair advantage, and yet Paz, whose political liberalism and advocacy of artistic freedom earned him the opprobrium of many of his fanatical contemporaries, was eventually proved right in several key respects. The Soviet regime proved to be closer to hell on earth than the paradise obstinately imagined by Neruda, and of all the latter's poetry it is the political verse, so crude in its urgings, so linguistically impoverished and often so narrowly tied to specific times and places, that today receives least attention both from academics and the wider reading public who, like Neruda in 1933, continue to prefer dreams to armoured trains.

By 1941 the Siqueiros incident had blown over, but Neruda's political views and interventions continued to get him into trouble both in Mexico and back home. At times he was blameless, such as when he founded a journal, *Araucanía*, designed to promote Chilean culture in Mexico, only to be promptly admonished by the Ministry in Santiago for putting a picture of a Mapuche Indian woman on the cover, since the image supposedly portrayed Chile as a country of savages. On other occasions he was deliberately provocative. In September of that year, he wrote 'Canto a Stalingrado' ('Song to Stalingrad') in honour of the Soviet troops defending the city against the Nazi invaders, and had hundreds of copies pasted up all over the Mexican capital. The gesture provoked considerable controversy in the press, to which Neruda's response was a 'Nuevo canto de amor a Stalingrado' ('A New Love Song to Stalingrad'), in which he again renounced the pessimism, self-obsession and excessive literariness of his early poetry in favour of a heartfelt 'grito de amor' ('cry of love') to the besieged city.[14] His stentorian proclamations eventually elicited a less genteel reaction. The details remain hazy, but it seems that during a trip to the neighbouring town of Cuernavaca on 29 December 1941 Neruda and his party were accosted by a group of German Nazis who had overheard them championing the Allied cause over lunch. He emerged with a head wound that required hospital treatment. The attack was, of course, unforgivable, though Neruda's aggressive insistence on bringing his poetry and his politics 'into the street' was never going to meet with unanimous approval, and he could hardly expect his endless taunts and provocations to go unanswered.

In 1942 Neruda made his first trip to Cuba, establishing a link that – surprisingly, given the course that Cuban history was to take

– would prove to be the source of considerable difficulties and disappointments. Ironically, this was to prove his happiest visit to the island, then governed by future dictator Fulgencio Batista. Neruda devoted most of his stay to collecting rare shells, but he saw enough of Batista's regime to be impressed, since in 1944 he wrote a fulsome 'Saludo a Batista' ('Salute to Batista'), published in the Chilean communist newspaper *El Siglo*, in which he referred to the Cuban leader as a true 'man of the people', a 'total American'.[15] It would be unfair to blame Neruda for a lack of foresight, since at the time Batista successfully presented himself as an out-and-out populist (he had legalized the Communist Party, which helped bring him to power in 1940). Still, it is interesting to note that Hernán Loyola saw fit to omit this 'incongruous' piece from his recent edition of Neruda's supposedly complete works.

The final straw in the increasingly precarious balancing act between his dual roles as diplomat and poet came in mid-1943, when Neruda, again without his government's permission, tried to persuade Brazilian dictator Getúlio Vargas to free imprisoned revolutionary leader Luis Carlos Prestes, so that the latter could attend his mother's funeral in Mexico. Vargas refused, and his refusal met with Neruda's standard response, the poem 'Dura elegía' ('Harsh Elegy'), which he recited at the funeral ceremony and in which he describes the 'little tyrant' as a bat and a thieving rat – an understandable, if not terribly diplomatic reaction.[16] Needless to say, the Brazilian Ambassador was less than overjoyed, and made an official protest to the Chilean government. Neruda defended his position, attempting to make a clear distinction between his official duties as Consul General of Chile and his ethical imperative as a writer, though his remarks, published in part in the Mexican daily *Excelsior*, were tantamount to a professional suicide note. As if in acknowledgement of this, he requested six months' leave, after which he did not return to the diplomatic service for more than twenty years. Just before leaving Mexico, Neruda, who had been granted a divorce from Maruca in February, finally married Delia on 2 July 1943 in a civil service in the town of Tetecala in the southwestern state of Michoacán. Their marriage certificate is pure fiction (Delia is said to be forty-five whereas in fact she was approaching sixty) but no one seems to have minded. There was also time for one more important public ceremony. On 17 August the University of Michoacán awarded Neruda his first honorary doctorate. His acceptance speech constitutes his first major 'Americanist' statement:

> How often I've thought that, whilst we know exactly where Mexico begins, we have no real idea of where it ends. The skin of America, the turbulent flesh of our America, starts at the Rio Grande, forms a waist in Central America, where two seas shower the burning palm trees with their spume, then broadens into a great pair of haunches, is suddenly broken apart by our main river, the thunderous Amazon, father of all rivers, it rises in blocks of diamond and silver in solar Peru, stretches out like a fertile womb over our Argentine pampas, and ends up crumbling to pieces in my homeland beyond the Straits of Magellan, beyond the final, freezing lands of the continent and the world, amidst the Antarctic waves.
>
> Yes, Mexico's skin flows and spreads, is severed and rises up, runs hot and cold, but it is the skin of America itself, the same dark crust beneath which the same fires glow, the same waters run and our common language scatters its seed.[17]

The reference to *our* America is surely a conscious echo of the famous essay of the same title by Cuban poet and freedom fighter José Martí (1853–1895), to whom Neruda would dedicate a poem in *Canto general* and who advocated a global, inclusive vision of Latin America that prefigures his own and was itself modelled on that of the continent's great Liberator, Simón Bolívar.

With second wife
Delia del Carril,
1943.

This already keen sense of Latin America as a cultural and
linguistic confederacy was further strengthened over the following
months, during which Neruda and Delia travelled widely on their
way back to Chile. They visited Panama and Colombia where,
besides giving further recitals, Neruda made several similar public
rallying cries for American unity. By far their most important port
of call, though, proved to be Peru. There, in October 1943, Neruda
visited the ancient Inca city of Machu Picchu, perched high in the
Andes. Though in a very different way, the experience was to have

as profound an effect on him as the outbreak of the Spanish Civil War had seven years previously. His initial reaction, however, was less than oracular. According to some sources, he enthusiastically declared the site a 'fantastic place for a barbecue'. Sympathetic biographers such as Adam Feinstein argue that 'this flippant remark . . . was a device to conceal the depth of his response', though given Neruda's penchant for Rabelaisian gourmandizing it is perfectly possible that it was meant seriously.[18] Anecdotes aside, what precisely was the significance of the ascent to Macchu Picchu, and how does this translate into 'Alturas de Macchu Picchu' ('Heights of Macchu Picchu'; the poet himself added the extra, prettifying 'c') that Neruda composed a full two years later and which many consider to be his greatest poem? This is what the poet himself had to say in 1954:

> After seeing the ruins at Macchu Picchu, the fabulous cultures of antiquity seemed to be made of cardboard, papier mâché . . . I could no longer separate myself from those constructions. I understood that, if we trod the same, hereditary soil, we had something to do with those lofty efforts of the American community, that we could not ignore them, that our ignorance or silence were not merely a crime but the continuation of a defeat . . . I thought about ancient American man. I thought about his ancient struggles intermeshed with present struggles. That was where the seeds of my idea for an American *Canto general* began to germinate . . . Now I saw the whole of America from the heights of Macchu Picchu.[19]

Machu Picchu, then, was the place where the fragments of Neruda's emergent Americanist vision finally coalesced, where he gained an overarching sense of historical development and continuity that had previously been lacking. Accordingly, the resulting poem takes the form of an anabasis both literal and symbolic, as the trek up to the ruins is simultaneously depicted as a spiritual ascent. Divided into twelve sections, it opens with what turns out to be a densely metaphorized, retrospective synopsis of the whole experience, initially described, in anticipation of the flurry of telluric images that permeate the remainder of the poem, as a rejuvenating descent into 'the genital quick of the earth' rather than a climb to the rarefied heights.[20] The next four sections plunge us back into the past, revisiting, for what would be the final time, the dark, death-ravaged world of *Residencia en la tierra*. Via a series of sometimes explicit allusions to the *Residencia* poems, the poet grapples with a fundamental existential problem, namely, the seemingly unbridgeable divide between the world of Nature and that of human history. The permanence of the former, achieved through repeated cycles of spontaneous self-renewal, is contrasted with the discontinuities of the latter, marked by countless individual deaths with no 'eternal, fathomless vein' to underpin them.[21] Machu Picchu seems to resolve the dilemma. When the poet reaches the citadel in the sixth section, his expression becomes ringingly prophetic, almost liturgical, celebrating a world where Humankind and Nature were as one, 'the cradle of lightning and of man'. Here, he trumpets, the feet of eagles and the feet of men walked together.[22] That particular description echoes a similar passage in an earlier 'conversion' poem, 'Reunión bajo nuevas banderas' ('Gathering under New Flags'), in which the poet, emerging from his dark night of the soul, pledged to 'join my wolf's steps' to 'the steps of men'.[23] Yet the euphoria is short-lived. After all, did not Machu Picchu too crumble and fall? The next two sections mull over this question, trying to establish precisely what it is that endures in the ruins, to decipher the shattered stone glyphs. They are followed by the remarkable ninth section, a paratactic piling up of eighty-one metaphors that visibly reconstructs the ruined city as an imposing column of words. It is the next section, however, that is pivotal. Here the still exultant poet suddenly interrupts his reverie to ask whether life at Machu Picchu was really any different from contemporary life, so damningly portrayed in the early sections of the poem. Did not people there suffer, freeze, starve and die, just as they do in modern cities? If so, has he not simply been fantasizing? These are crucial questions and, tellingly, the poet elects not to tackle them. Instead, as Enrico Mario Santí puts it, he 'leap[s] over the conceptual problems that are entailed in the previous demystification . . . for the alternative of a vision'.[24] A diffuse, often obscure penultimate section gives way to evangelical tub-thumping in the closing lines, as the poet presumptuously declares that he – and his poem – is the privileged conduit through which Machu Picchu will live on, thereby allowing the past to be preserved in the present:

> *Apegadme los cuerpos como imanes.*
> *Acudid a mis venas y a mi boca.*
> *Hablad por mis palabras y mi sangre.*

> Fasten your bodies to me like magnets.
> Hasten to my veins and my mouth.
> Speak through my words and my blood.[25]

In the light of the unanswered questions of the tenth section, this may strike more exigent readers as the most fudged of epiphanies. Yet why does Neruda insist on foisting this distorted vision on the ruins? The answer surely lies in the development of his political thinking between his visit to Machu Picchu and the composition of the poem, during which time he had joined the Communist Party and subscribed to the Marxist-Leninist view of historical progress. When collective utopia is the prize, any number of individual lives are worth sacrificing for it; it matters little how many poor souls shivered and went hungry at Machu Picchu, since they did so – albeit unwittingly – so that centuries later the rebellious masses could carry out the socialist revolution. This, then, is the continuity that Neruda espied up on the mountain fastnesses. It is predicated on a calamitous incapacity or refusal to differentiate the fate of flesh-and-blood individuals from that of the bloodless abstraction Mankind, a misprision that led to the sort of atrocities that blighted the twentieth century and news of which would later shake Neruda's faith in the communist dream to the core. In the present case it is also grounded on a basic historical misunderstanding. Though he primarily champions the common folk of Machu Picchu, Neruda's portrayal of the ancient Amerindian world is ludicrously sanitized. The Inca Empire was despotic and fuelled by fear. Slavery was commonplace, its citizens had few basic freedoms and the spectre of death – in the forms of war and bloody human sacrifice – loomed large. Significantly, Neruda also downplays the cruelty of the prehispanic world in poems such as 'Los hombres' ('Men'), where the Mayan ritual sacrifice of virgins is portrayed as just one more exotic rite of spring.[26] These excessively benign depictions may have been influenced by the ideas of José Carlos Mariátegui (1894–1930), political philosopher and founder of the Peruvian Socialist Party, who, in his influential *Siete ensayos de interpretación de la realidad peruana* ('Seven Interpretative Essays on Peruvian Reality'; 1928), had claimed, incorrectly, that early Inca society was proto-communist. Neruda was familiar with Mariátegui's thought (indeed, he mentioned him in a speech delivered just before his visit to the ruins) and its appeal is obvious, since, according to the Peruvian's schema, Machu Picchu, never reached by the Spanish conquistadors, was an emblematic locus of a primitive communism that would eventually re-emerge, after a series of Hegelian transformations, in the shape of the contemporary proletariat of which Neruda had appointed himself spokesman. No wonder everything seemed to make sense there. Still, even if Mariátegui's theory were sound, the celebration of a pure American spirit untainted by

Spanish colonialism remains deeply problematic, given that the *Latin* America that emerged from the Spanish conquest was predominantly *mestizo* or mixed, an ethnic melting pot in which Indian communities, themselves highly diverse, constituted but one, invariably marginalized element, the section of society, in fact, least likely to benefit from a popular revolution. How could pristine Machu Picchu possibly symbolize or even meaningfully relate to all of *that*? I have dwelt so long on this poem and its genesis not only because it constitutes a critical turning point in Neruda's life and work, but also because, if scrutinized closely and dispassionately, it reveals a number of lacunae and inconsistencies that would resurface in much of his later political verse, but to which its forceful rhetoric and rousing finale can easily blind us.

As I have already indicated, once back in Chile Neruda's most important action was formally to join the Communist Party. Even before he had done so, however, he was persuaded to stand for the

The ancient Inca citadel at Machu Picchu, inspiration for one of Neruda's most famous poems.

Senate as representative of the harsh, grindingly poor northern mining provinces of Antofagasta and Tarapacá, a position to which he was duly elected on 4 March 1945, after a campaign which had brought him into contact with the most destitute and ruthlessly exploited of his countrymen. His experiences in the mining communities, movingly recounted in the poem 'Saludo al norte' ('Salute to the North'; 1945) and the speech 'Journey to the North' (1946), further reinforced both his political convictions, which by then were undisguisedly Stalinist, and his conception of the poet as servant and representative of his people.[27] Then, on 27 June 1946, president Juan Antonio Ríos died in office. Shortly afterwards, Neruda was asked to act as chief of propaganda for the electoral campaign of Radical Party candidate Gabriel González Videla. González Videla appeared sympathetic towards the Left and promised the Communists seats in his cabinet in return for their support. On 4 September he won a close-run election. Almost immediately, a series of major strikes broke out, principally in the mining fields of the north. With the threat of a crippling general strike looming, González Videla declared a state of siege. It was during this uneasy stand-off between government and workers, the last period of relative peace and stability that Neruda would experience for many years, that the final volume in the *Residencia* series, *Tercera residencia* ('Third Residence'), appeared. The work is a fascinating if deeply disjointed miscellany, juxtaposing typically sombre pieces composed in the early 1930s with the impassioned protest poetry of *España en el corazón*, which is included complete, and the first overtly Americanist poems, such as 'Un canto para Bolívar' ('A Song for Bolívar'), which he had written in Mexico. A note appended to 'Las furias y las penas' explains the discrepancy:

This poem was written in 1934. How many things have happened in the meantime! Spain, where I wrote it, is a girdle of ruins. Ah! If only with a single drop of poetry or love we could assuage the world's anger, but that can only be achieved through struggle and the heart's resolve.

The world has changed and my poetry has changed with it. A drop of blood fallen on these lines will live on with them, as indelible as love.[28]

In fact, his world was about to change again, and just as traumatically. The partial truce crumbled and industrial action resumed apace, culminating in a massive but entirely legal coal miners' strike in the southern city of Lota in October 1947, which González Videla, now aligning himself firmly with the US in the incipient Cold War (that same year he broke off diplomatic ties with the Soviet Union, Yugoslavia and Czechoslovakia), falsely claimed was part of a Communist Party plot orchestrated from Moscow, and in response to which he stubbornly refused to negotiate. Instead, he sacked the three Communist members of his cabinet, took advantage of 'extraordinary powers' conferred on him by Congress and broke up the strike by force, arresting hundreds of miners and sending many more first to military prisons and later to a brutal detention camp in the northern desert town of Pisagua, which for a time was overseen by Chile's future dictator, Augusto Pinochet, whose coup d'état in 1973 would cast a grim shadow over Neruda's final days. Those were the first in a series of often violent measures that would culminate in the decree in September 1948 of the farcically named 'Law for the Permanent Defence of Democracy' (popularly referred to as the 'Ley Maldita' or 'Accursed Law'), which outlawed the Communist Party and summarily struck thousands of 'subversives' from the electoral roll. For the Left, it was a galling volte-face. In typically pugnacious fashion, Neruda turned on the president in the form of a virulent newspaper article ironically titled 'An Intimate Letter for Millions of Men', published in Venezuela and Mexico in November and December 1947.[29] In this at once coolly argued and recklessly courageous piece, which, politically speaking, left him in a completely untenable position, he accused González Videla of betraying his people on every conceivable front and identified his regime as a sinister stepping-stone in a US-led plan to hijack the democracies of Latin America. The president's immediate retort was a formal request that Neruda's senatorial status be revoked, a move that would strip him of his political immunity and allow him to be arrested. Undeterred, on 6 January 1948 Neruda launched an even more blistering verbal assault in the Senate, in a speech which, after Zola, he titled 'Yo acuso' ('J'accuse'). As well as lashing out repeatedly at González Videla, he read out

The poet as senator, addressing a political rally in Chile, mid-1940s.

the names of 628 prisoners detained at Pisagua.[30] The president had heard enough. Neruda now became a marked man (one national newspaper even offered a reward for his arrest), and it was clear that he must either leave the country or immediately go into hiding.

The fourteen-month period from January 1948 to March 1949 constitutes perhaps the most remarkable interlude in what was already a quite extraordinary life. During that time, aided by the Chilean Communist Party and its various representatives, as well as by loyal friends willing to put their livelihood in danger, Neruda and Delia went underground, constantly changing address in order to evade the clutches of the police. Fittingly, one of those who housed Neruda, and who was subsequently instrumental in his escape from Chile, was Spaniard Víctor Pey, who had arrived in Chile on the *Winnipeg* a decade earlier. Years later, in his memoirs, González Videla claimed that he could have had Neruda arrested at the drop of a hat but chose not to do so in order not to make a popular hero out of him.[31] Such a claim seems highly unlikely, as to have bagged a scalp as big as Neruda's would have constituted a significant coup for the regime. In the midst of the daily drama, and using whatever source materials he had to hand, Neruda somehow managed to compose most of the *Canto general*. He also managed to make astonishingly labyrinthine arrangements for its eventual publication, sending *cantos* or sets of *cantos* to a vast network of collaborators to be reassembled later. In addition, he found time to put together an apocryphal *Popular Anthology*, which consisted largely of obscene poems attacking González Videla supposedly written by a number of poets, all of whom are in fact Neruda in disguise. This he had circulated in pamphlet form.

During the tense months in hiding, various plans were hatched to smuggle him out of the country, but after much deliberation it was decided that the safest escape route would be across the Andes to Argentina, a journey that would have to be undertaken on horseback. Neruda would recall this hazardous trek, begun in early March 1949, in exalted, near mystical tones in his Nobel Prize acceptance speech in 1971, which often reads like a Romantic travelogue, full of rapt descriptions of the landscape and its exotic inhabitants. However, one of his fellow travellers, Víctor Bianchi, tells a rather different tale. By the time it came to leave, Neruda, never a waif, was grossly overweight, having kept up his spirits during his enforced confinement by constant banqueting, washing down his feasts with endless draughts of red wine and whisky. He was barely able to mount his horse, and Bianchi describes him variously as a bearded sack of potatoes and a panting, flaccid seal.[32] Nevertheless, he somehow made it to the Argentine town of San Martín de los Andes, where he was met by Party members who escorted him to Buenos Aires.

Despite all his travails, Neruda never lost sight of his primary goal, the publication of the *Canto general*, veiled references to which appear in a number of the letters he sent to Delia, who had remained behind in Santiago, and a typescript of which, bearing the false title *Risas y lágrimas* ('Laughter and Tears') by one Benigno Espinoza, he had taken with him on his epic journey. It eventually appeared in two separate editions. The first, a luxury printing of just 500 copies, with illustrations by Rivera and Siqueiros, came out in Mexico in April 1950. The second, so-called clandestine edition, which bears a false Mexican imprimatur, appeared in Chile that same year, as the culmination of one of the most remarkable underground publishing operations ever undertaken.[33] It is strikingly illustrated by Chilean painter and engraver José Venturelli and contains a defiant preface by Secretary General of the Chilean Communist Party, Galo González, lauding the book as the loftiest achievement of 'our greatest engineer of human souls' (the chilling formulation is Stalin's). Running to more than fifteen thousand lines, *Canto general* is by far Neruda's most ambitious work, though whether it is his greatest is very much open to question. It presents itself as a vast, poetic chronicle of the history of Latin America from pre-Columbian times to the present, an aim unambiguously spelled out in the opening poem, 'Amor América', which includes the lapidary declaration 'I am here to recount history'.[34] The enterprise was not without precedents, which date back as far as Alonso de Ercilla y Zúñiga's epic poem *La Araucana* (1574). Later came the patriotic odes and civic poems of Venezuelan Andrés Bello (1781–1865), Ecuadorian José Joaquín de Olmedo (1780–1847) and Cuban José María Heredia (1803–1839), followed by the bullishly chauvinistic poetry of Peruvian José Santos Chocano (1875–1934) and Uruguayan Álvaro Armando Vasseur (1878–1969), who published his *Cantos del Nuevo Mundo* ('Songs of the New World') in 1907. Then there was Neruda's early hero Sabat Ercasty, whose *Pantheos* (1917) is an ecstatic paean to the New World, and who later penned hymns to many of the same national heroes later celebrated by his young admirer. Even arch-aesthete Rubén Darío had tried his hand at patriotic sabre-rattling in poems such as 'Salutación del optimista' ('The Optimist's Greeting') and 'A Roosevelt'.[35] Perhaps the most important forerunner of the *Canto general*, however, was Anglo- rather than Latin American. I am referring to Walt Whitman (1819–1892), who was well known to Darío and Sabat, translated and slavishly imitated by Vasseur, and is directly invoked by Neruda, who had long since admired his poetry, in the ninth section of the *Canto*, 'Que despierte el leñador' ('Let the Rail Splitter Awake'). None of these poets, however, with the possible exception of Whitman, came close to Neruda's immense sweep, and none of their visions was underwritten by his unwavering if highly questionable central assumption: that the true hero of the American epic was the common people who one day would definitively liberate the continent through a Marxist revolution. As Enrico Mario Santí puts it, the work starts out as a 'modern, secular analogy of a sacred book', with the poet-chronicler depicting prehispanic America as a Garden of Eden and cataloguing the flora, fauna and the early Amerindian cultures that populated it.[36]

A bearded Neruda during his final days in hiding, preparing his escape to
Argentina across the Andes, 1949.

After the intercalated 'Alturas de Macchu Picchu', which effectively explains how the whole project took shape, subsequent sections deal with the Spanish conquest, liberation movements from the sixteenth to the twentieth centuries (culminating, of course, in the rise of mass socialism), dictatorship and US neo-colonialism. With the sixth section, however, 'América, no invoco tu nombre en vano' ('America, I Do Not Invoke Your Name in Vain'), which does little more than tread familiar water, the book starts to run out of narrative steam. Section 7 is a self-contained 'Canto general de Chile', while section 8, 'La tierra se llama Juan' ('The Land's Name is Juan') is a sustained exercise in giving a voice to humble labourers and victims of social injustice, whose often harrowing stories might otherwise never be heard. Here, as the poet promised at the rhapsodic close of 'Alturas de Macchu Picchu', they really do get to speak through his words, as most of the poems take the form of what are made to look like spontaneous first-person accounts. Next comes 'Que despierte el leñador', a lengthy, unstinting attack on the US imperialism threatening wholesome, honest socialist values both abroad and at home, where McCarthy was busy hunting down communists such as Charlie Chaplin, whom the poet describes, perhaps a tad hyperbolically, as 'the ultimate father of tenderness in this world'.[37] The rail splitter of the title is Abraham Lincoln, to whose brotherly, democratic spirit the poet appeals in order to halt the depradations of the present. This sequence also contains Neruda's first, tremblingly reverent eulogy to Stalin. The flattery clearly worked, as the poem earned Neruda a Soviet-sponsored International Peace Prize in 1950, an honour which he shared with Pablo Picasso and that same Paul Robeson whose records he had listened to with Josie Bliss in what by then must have seemed a very distant past. There follow 'El fugitivo' ('The Fugitive'), a largely autobiographical section dealing with his days in hiding, and 'Las flores de Punitaqui' ('The Flowers of Punitaqui'), written as early as 1946, which reflects on the time Neruda spent campaigning in the impoverished mining communities of the north. Section 12, 'Los ríos del canto' ('The Rivers of Song'), consists of five verse letters to friends living and dead – Venezuelan novelist Miguel Otero Silva (1908–1985), Rafael Alberti, Argentine poet José González Carbalho (1899–1958), Mexican composer Silvestre Revueltas (1899–1940) and Miguel Hernández – while the angry 'Coral del Año Nuevo para la patria en tinieblas' ('New Year Chorale for the Benighted Homeland') returns to contemporary Chilean issues. The almost totally incongruous fourteenth canto, 'El gran océano' ('The Great Ocean'), deals in baroque detail with the marine life of the continent, and the work then concludes with 'Yo soy' ('I Am'), Neruda's first, intriguing attempt at poetic autobiography, which includes a touching poem, 'Disposiciones' ('Instructions'), in which he asks to be buried at his beloved Isla Negra:

Compañeros, enterradme en Isla Negra,
frente al mar que conozco, a cada área rugosa
de piedras y de olas que mis ojos perdidos
no volverán a ver.
[...]
Saben
que allí quiero dormir entre los párpados
del mar y de la tierra ...[38]

Friends, bury me at Isla Negra,
opposite the sea that I know, opposite every wrinkled stretch
of stones and waves that my vanished eyes
will never see again.
[...]
You know
that is where I want to sleep between the eyelids
of sea and earth ...

The poem presents itself as a last will and testament and, given the precariousness of the circumstances in which it was composed, Neruda may actually have intended it as such, though even if he did not, it certainly helps to heighten the drama of the closing pages. All that holds the disparate later sections together is a sporadically repeated series of stock metaphors that pepper the entire work and which depict the common people of Latin America as a manifold unity. Chief among these are the tree, with its tangle of roots and branches, and the river with its network of tributaries. The former first appears in the fourth section, 'Los libertadores' ('The Liberators'), which triumphantly introduces the people as protagonist:

Aquí viene el árbol, el árbol
de la tormenta, el árbol del pueblo.
De la tierra suben los héroes
como las hojas por la savia,
y el viento estrella los follajes
de muchedumbre rumorosa,
hasta que cae la semilla
del pan otra vez a la tierra.[39]

Here comes the tree, the tree
of turmoil, the tree of the people.
Its heroes rise from the earth
like leaves from the sap,
and the wind spangles
the murmuring multitude's foliage,
until the seed falls
once more from bread to the earth.

One obvious reason for the book's increasingly shaky structure are the extreme circumstances in which much of it was written, though we should also bear in mind that the project as a whole took more than a decade to come together and that entire sections of it were written well before Neruda had a clear idea of how the finished work might look. The *Canto general* polarized the critics as never before.[40] For those already converted to the cause, it was a revolutionary bible; indeed, an annotated copy was found among the possessions of Che Guevara after he was shot dead in Bolivia in 1967. For others, however, including some of Neruda's closest friends, the constant proselytizing and the insistently vituperative tone constituted grave weaknesses. Tomás Lago, for example, warned him during early readings that the targets of his vitriol were too localized and transitory for the poetry to last.[41] The observation was a shrewd one, since many of the poems now appear as little more than lifeless relics incapable of engaging a contemporary reader. Particularly illustrative in this respect are the frequent potshots at González Videla. Consider the following lines from 'González Videla, el traidor de Chile' ('González Videla, Betrayer of Chile'):

Es González Videla la rata que sacude
su pelambrera llena de estiércol y de sangre
sobre la tierra mía que vendió. Cada día
saca de sus bolsillos las monedas robadas
y piensa si mañana venderá territorio o sangre.
[...]
                    Triste clown, *miserable*
mezcla de mono y rata, cuyo rabo
peinan en Wall Street con pomada de oro,
no pasarán los días sin que caigas del árbol
y seas el montón de inmundicia evidente
que el transeúnte evita pisar en las esquinas![42]

González Videla is the rat who shakes
his coat caked with dung and blood

over this land of mine which he has sold. Every day
he pulls stolen coins from his pockets
wondering whether tomorrow he will sell land or blood.
[. . .]
                    Miserable *clown*, wretched
cross between a monkey and a rat, whose tail
they comb on Wall Street with gilded pomade,
it won't be long now before you fall from your tree
and become a conspicuous mound of filth
which pedestrians try not to step in as they round the corner!

Even if we choose to overlook the banality of the imagery, the
excruciating hollowness of the rhetoric and the absence of any
meaningful content, the lack of proper focus remains striking.
González Videla was not a particularly pleasant man, but as Latin
American dictators go he was something of a pussycat. The uninformed reader might think him as evil as the likes of Venezuela's
Juan Vicente Gómez (1857–1935) or the Dominican Republic's
Rafael Leonidas Trujillo (1891–1961), both of whom also receive
a tongue-lashing, but when it came to heinous, arbitrary acts of
violence, he was simply not in their league. Today he scarcely
merits a mention in the annals of Latin American despotism,
but Neruda's proximity to events caused him to blow González
Videla's importance out of all proportion. Although, as I have
already suggested, when it came to political poetry Neruda was
a much greater eulogist than he was a denigrator, even the cele-
bratory verse of the *Canto general* is not without its shortcomings.
For example, whenever Neruda is praising his beloved *pueblo* he
switches automatically to 'organicist' mode, unleashing a torrent
of metaphors (tree, river, roots, stone, metal, mineral, wheat,
seeds, light and so on) all of which ultimately derive from that
deep-seated equation of Man and Nature that he made at Machu
Picchu, and which are designed to portray the proletariat as the

immovable bedrock of history. Ironically, their repetitiveness
and predictability give them a decidedly mechanical feel. One
might also question Neruda's resolutely blinkered optimism.
The picture he paints of Latin American history is a consistently
dark one, punctuated intermittently by the feeblest rays of hope.
Consequently, his dogged insistence on presenting it as a steadily
unfolding narrative of progress makes many of the more jubilant
poems ring painfully false. Take for example 'El pueblo victorioso'
('The People Victorious'), the penultimate poem in the suggestively
lengthy section 5, 'La arena traicionada' ('The Soil Betrayed'),
which traces a hundred-year history of tyranny and oppression.
After an horrendous litany of demagoguery, corruption and blood-
shed that shows no sign of abating, the poet suddenly announces:

> *Mi pueblo vencerá. Todos los pueblos*
> *vencerán, uno a uno.*
> [...]
> *La hora de la victoria está cerca.*[43]

> My people will win. All peoples
> Will win, one by one.
> [...]
> The hour of victory is near.

However much we may admire his resilience, nothing we have
read in the rest of this section could lead us to this hopelessly naive
conclusion. Ironically, the most memorable poems in the *Canto
general* are the least political. Both the 'Canto general de Chile' and,
supremely, 'El gran océano' contain some of Neruda's greatest nature
poetry, as well as fine meditative pieces such as 'Melancolía cerca
de Orizaba' ('Melancholy Near Orizaba'), in which the poet, during
his stay in Mexico, recalls his Chilean roots.[44] Similarly, many of
the poems in 'Yo soy' that look back to Neruda's childhood and

Frontispiece and opening lines of the original, corrected typescript of 'Los
Libertadores', the fourth section of *Canto general* (1950). Note how Neruda,
almost certainly on Delia's recommendation, has repeatedly crossed out the
word 'raíces' ('roots'), which he was prone to overuse.

Este es el arbol de los libres .
El arbol tierra,el arbol nube.
el arbol pan,el arbol flecha,
el arbol puño,el arbol fuego.
No ahoga el agua tormentosa
de nuestra época nocturna,
~~peree~~ su ~~alta radiante~~ *balancea*
~~balancea~~ su poderío,
otras veces de nuevo caen
~~que~~ ramas rotas por la cólera
y ~~la~~ ceniza amenazante
cubre su antigua majestad:
así pasó desde otros tiempos,
así salió de la agonía,
hasta que una mano secreta,
unos brazos innumerables,
el pueblo,guardaba ~~raíces~~,
escondía troncos inmensos,
y sus labios eran las hojas
del inmenso arbol ~~~~
~~derramado por~~ todas partes,
caminando con sus raíces.

Este es el arbol,el arbol
del pueblo,de todos los pueblos,
de la libertad,de la lucha.
Asómate a ~~xxx~~ su cabellera,
toca sus rayos renovados,
~~mete~~ la mano en las usinas
donde su fruto palpitante
~~su luz propaga~~ cada día,
levanta esta tierra en tus manos
participa de este esplendor,
toma tu pan y tu manzana,
tu ~~cuaderno,tu corazón~~
tu *corazón* y tu caballo
y monta guardia en la frontera
en el límite de sus hojas,
defiende el fin de sus ~~raíces~~,
comparte las noches hostiles,
vigila el ciclo de la aurora,
~~sonríe~~ la altura estrellada,
y vamos ~~al~~ árbol,el árbol
que crece en medio de la tierra.

adolescence, as well as recalling his early adventures in both love and poetry, are captivating, so much so that we feel distinctly short-changed when we return to the cloying psalmodizing of 'A mi partido' ('To My Party'), a fulsome gloss on Aragon's 'Du Poète à son parti' (1944).[45] Neruda himself attempted to justify the undeniable jadedness, even banality of much of the language of the *Canto general* by claiming that he had made a conscious decision to write as a chronicler rather than a poet. It had, he stressed, been xtremely difficult for him to curb his natural lyrical impulse in order to achieve the desired effect, though even the most sympathetic reader must often wonder whether it was worth the effort.[46]

What are we to conclude? As Enrico Mario Santí suggests, love it or loathe it, we ought at least to concede that *Canto general* is an *important* book, a milestone in modern Latin American letters.[47] That was the line taken even by writers such as the Argentine Julio Cortázar (1914–1984), whose own late conversion to socialism was every bit as dramatic and uncompromising as Neruda's, but who continued to believe that, for both aesthetic and ethical reasons, 'revolutionary literature' (experimental works of unconstrained imagination) should take precedence over 'literature of the revolution' (conventionally written works that toe the party line).[48] In both his 'Open Letter to Pablo Neruda' (1971) and the obituary 'Neruda Amongst Us' (1973), whilst recognizing the generosity of spirit of the *Canto general* and the worthiness of its intentions, Cortázar cites *Residencia en la tierra* as Neruda's most significant achievement.[49] Indeed, he goes as far as to suggest that the anguished plumbing of the human condition in the earlier book offers a critique more radical than any to be found in the later work, in which Neruda has ceased to ask probing existential questions in favour of making blanket political recommendations. After all, Cortázar asks, if one does not first know what Man is essentially, on what grounds can one advise him how to vote? Many other creative writers and intellectuals, on both the right and the left, felt precisely the same way: one could readily admire the *Canto general*, but it was difficult to love it. Ironically, one of the most even-handed summaries of a deeply uneven book was provided by Neruda's arch-rival, Octavio Paz:

> [*Canto general*] is a huge cauldron which contains all sorts of things: dip in a hand and out come quartz birds, whistling feathers, iridescent shells, rusty pistols, broken knives, shattered idols. Harangues, diatribes, mile after mile of platitudes and then suddenly, without warning, luminous and exhilarating, handfuls of recently gathered splendours, intact and still full of life.[50]

Unsurprisingly, Paz preferred the book's poetic flights of fancy to the leaden longueurs of its political pamphleteering. Nevertheless, it was the latter that was to dominate Neruda's poetry over the following years, during which both his political and aesthetic sectarianism would reach disquieting, often unpalatable extremes.

5

Love and Politics

Neruda's eventual emergence from his period in hiding was every bit as theatrical as his initial disappearance and his clandestine toings and froings. Despite having made it to Buenos Aires he was still in danger, as the Argentine police had orders to arrest him. As luck would have it, his friend Miguel Ángel Asturias was now working in the Guatemalan Embassy. The two men were not dissimilar physically (according to Neruda, they both looked like fattened turkeys) and so Asturias offered Neruda his passport, a ruse that worked a treat in Montevideo but was less likely to impress the French authorities, who finally let Neruda into the country only after Pablo Picasso had intervened strenuously on his behalf. His first public appearance was a memorable one. He turned up at the Salle Pleyel in Paris for the closing session of the World Congress for the Forces for Peace (another Soviet concoction), where, before a dumbstruck audience that included Paul Éluard, Louis Aragon, Paul Robeson and Picasso, he apologized for his delay in getting there and, without further ado, recited 'Un canto para Bolívar'. It was quite an entrance, though by then one would have expected nothing less of him. Shortly afterwards, in June, he made his first, eagerly awaited trip to the Soviet Union. Shown only what the authorities deemed fit for inspection, and loudly fêted at every turn, Neruda, like Vallejo (who made two starry-eyed trips to the USSR in 1928–9), Alberti and Hernández before him, was convinced that he had set foot in the Promised Land. His stay, which was followed by visits to Poland and Hungary, persuaded him that his poetic expression, already greatly simplified in much of the *Canto general*, had to be pared down still further if it was to be fully accessible to its intended readership, the working masses. That led him to take a drastic and highly controversial decision. When his Hungarian translators were preparing an edition of his collected works, he instructed them to exclude *Residencia en la tierra*, which he had come to view as dangerously defeatist poetry, singularly ill-equipped for the urgent task in hand of building a bright, socialist future. He extended this self-censorship to future editions in Spanish, which he urged should be re-edited accordingly. Fortunately, *Residencia* was never excised from his complete works in his mother tongue. The late 1940s and the first half of the 1950s constitute the period of Neruda's most extreme political and artistic militancy, and both his pronouncements on aesthetics and much of the poetry that he composed during those years make for profoundly depressing reading. Feinstein says that Neruda, ever distrustful of prescriptive artistic creeds and trends, never subscribed to the precepts of socialist realism outlined by Andrei Zhdanov at the first Soviet Writers' Congress in 1934.[1] Nevertheless, while he may have made no formal declaration of support for those principles, he undoubtedly put them into practice, as we shall soon see.

After further stops in Romania and Prague, in late August Pablo and Delia headed for Mexico, Chile still being out of bounds. It was there, in a speech delivered to the Latin American Peace Congress on 18 September, that he made public his decision to renounce his early verse, taking time out to condemn bourgeois filth such as Eliot, Rilke, Kafka and Sartre (!), proponents one and all of a self-indulgent pessimism that was no more than a symptom of the ineluctable decline of their moribund class.[2] At the same time, he fell over himself to extol that great 'poet' Mao Tse-tung. Just for good measure, he threw in a dig at his 'friend' the novelist José Revueltas (1914–1976), brother of composer Silvestre, whose recently published novel *Los días terrenales* (Days on Earth) he dismissed as an anti-communist work full of 'the poison of a bygone age' and 'destructive mysticism'. Such rash comments are a good indicator of the extent of Neruda's own ideological short-sightedness, since the novel does not oppose communism *per se*, but rather the self-serving and exploitative acts all too often perpet-rated in its name. Perhaps Neruda's bile was partly provoked by the state of his health, since he was suffering from phlebitis, an excruciatingly painful swelling of the veins in the legs, which left him bed-ridden. In a letter to Neruda's half-sister Laura, Delia attributed the illness to his prolonged period of near total inactivity when in hiding, though rather than laying the blame at the door of González Videla, she should probably have laid it at the bottom of a whisky bottle.[3] Phlebitis is a classic drinker's affliction and, during that period of repeated upheaval, drinking – alongside poetry – had remained one of the few constants in Neruda's life. In fact, there had been no let-up on that front since the bohemian nights in Spain with Lorca and entourage. The years as Consul in Mexico in particular seem to have drifted by in a steady haze. Delia could and often did tut and wag her finger, but she was powerless to curb his excesses; besides, her unconditional love for her husband made her unwilling to kick up a serious fuss. Neruda's state of prostration did not stop him from overseeing the publication of the luxury edition of the *Canto general*, which appeared in March. Once he had recovered, he and Delia embarked on almost two years of frantic travelling, which would see them visit Guatemala, Paris, Prague, New Delhi (where he paid president Jawaharlal Nehru an official visit as representative of Partisans for Peace), Poland, East Germany, Romania, Mongolia, China (where he presented the Lenin Peace Prize to Soong Ching-Ling, widow of revolutionary leader Sun Yat-Sen, the so-called 'Father of modern China'), Austria and Switzerland until finally, in January 1952, they settled in Capri, where Italian historian Edwin Cerio offered them his villa. In July of that year, a book of passionate Spanish love poetry appeared in Naples. Published anonymously, it contained a foreword in the form of a letter by one Rosario de la Cerda, ostensibly its dedicatee, dated Havana, 31 October 1951, which explained the genesis and content of the volume. Its title was *Los versos del capitán* ('The Captain's Verses') and it concealed, though not particularly well, what by then was already a long, convoluted and ultimately very sad story. Rosario de la Cerda was in fact Matilde Urrutia (whose full name was Matilde *Rosario* Urrutia *Cerda*) and her poet Neruda himself, and the book marked the culmination of an affair that had started as far back as 1946, when a chance meeting in the house of a mutual friend, soprano and music teacher Blanca Hauser, had led to a brief and seemingly inconsequential fling. The pseudonym throws retrospective light on a bizarre aside from 'Que despierte el leñador' that had baffled critics several years earlier:

Paz para mi mano derecha,
que sólo quiere escribir Rosario.[4]

Peace for my right hand,
which wants only to write Rosario.

It was chance too that eventually reunited the couple. In 1950 Matilde was taking singing classes in Mexico City in the vain hope of reviving a flagging and decidedly sleazy career as a cabaret performer (according to some sources, as a means of supplementing her meagre income she had become involved in the trafficking and prostitution of Chilean girls in Peru in the early 1940s).[5] Somehow, she managed to wheedle her way into the poet's circle of friends, and when Neruda fell ill she was appointed to look after him, though she had no formal qualification in nursing. Their passion was quickly reignited, and from that moment on they grabbed every conceivable opportunity to be together, beginning with the trip to Guatemala, on which Matilde accompanied Pablo and Delia, supposedly in her 'official' capacity as his carer. However, it was in Europe that Neruda went to quite extraordinary lengths to engineer trysts with his new lover, frequently using his Communist Party links to secure visas for her. That, of course, meant deceiving Delia on a daily basis, and Neruda proved to be a heartless maestro of deception. Besides lying about his own sudden, occasionally prolonged absences, he would send her off on spurious missions so that he could spend time with Matilde. Delia's admiration for Neruda was undimmed, and she invariably acquiesced; indeed, it was while she was in Chile on one such assignment that Neruda moved Matilde into the villa in Capri, where they proceeded to behave like love-struck teenagers without a thought for the oblivious Delia, pointlessly traipsing halfway across the globe, well into her sixty-eighth year.

Ignoring for a moment the distasteful context in which they were written and published, how do *Los versos del capitán* measure up as poetry? The love poems are the most ardent that Neruda had composed in twenty years; indeed, their exuberance and intensity throw into painful relief the absence in his work of any such verse for Delia. The image repertoire closely resembles that of the *Veinte poemas de amor*, and there are several seemingly conscious allusions to the earlier collection. This is not surprising, since Matilde, like Neruda, was from the town of Chillán in southern Chile, a connection that inspired him to celebrate the love of his final years with the same potently sensuous language and imagery with which he had immortalized the muses of his youth. Thus her body is variously compared to wheat, grapes, roses, poppies, but especially – and repeatedly – to the fecund earth, in ways that clearly recall *Veinte poemas* 1:

> *Bella,*
> *no hay nada como tus caderas,*
> *tal vez la tierra tiene*

en algún sitio oculto
la curva y el aroma de tu cuerpo.[6]

Beautiful one,
there is nothing like your hips,
perhaps the earth has
in some hidden place
the contours and fragrance of your body.

Even more striking are the following lines from 'El Insecto' ('The Insect'), a sportive gloss on Baudelaire's 'La Géante' ('The Giantess'):

De tus caderas a tus pies
Quiero hacer un largo viaje.
[. . .]
Voy por estas colinas
[. . .]
Aquí hay una montaña.
No saldré nunca de ella.
Oh qué musgo tan gigante!
Y un cráter, una rosa
de fuego humedecido![7]

I want to make a long journey
from your hips to your feet.
[. . .]
I go along these hills.
[. . .]
Here is a mountain.
I'll never get over it.
Oh what a huge clump of moss!
And a crater, a rose
of moistened fire!

Here, as in *Veinte poemas* 13, the poet imagines himself as an insect scurrying over his lover's expectant body. What has changed is the tone. Gone are the aggression and sense of erotic rivalry in favour of playfulness and a new emphasis on shared pleasure. In the somewhat rambling 'Epitalamio' ('Epithalamium'), meanwhile, Neruda refers to his lover as his 'bienamada' ('beloved'), an epithet previously reserved for Josie Bliss (see chapter Two). The implication is that he has finally found someone to replace her in his affections, and we might reasonably interpret the poem as a whole as a rewriting or 'updating' of 'Juntos nosotros', the luxuriant wedding hymn for his Burmese princess. Yet there are other, less savoury matters addressed in the pages of *Los versos del capitán*. Many of the poems in the sections 'El deseo' ('Desire') and the ominously titled 'Las furias' ('Furies'; an echo, perhaps, of 'Las furias y la penas'?) deal with the uglier aspects of love, not least jealousy (to which Neruda was especially prone), resentment and recrimination. The tone can be harsh, cruel even, and occasionally threatening. There is also a further, far darker theme present. Matilde never bore Neruda a child; she did, however, have at least two miscarriages, and the story of one of them is recounted fragmentarily over the course of *Los versos del capitán*. The poem 'El hijo' ('The Child') clearly refers to her pregnancy and, looking down the list of subscribers to the first edition of the book, we see that the second copy has been reserved for Neruda Urrutia, the name he intended to give his son – the thought of having a(nother) daughter seems not to have occurred to him. By the time of 'La pródiga' ('The Profligate'), however, Matilde has obviously miscarried. Instead of consoling her, Neruda reproaches her in the most unspeakable fashion:

Devuélveme a mi hijo!

Lo has olvidado en las puertas
del placer, oh pródiga

enemiga,
has olvidado que viniste a esta cita,
la más profunda, aquella
en que los dos, unidos, seguiremos hablando,
por su boca, amor mío,
ay todo aquello
que no alcanzamos a decirnos?[8]

Give me back my child!

Have you forgotten him
at the doors of pleasure, oh profligate
enemy,
have you forgotten that you came to this tryst,
the deepest one, the one in which
the two of us, together, will go on saying
through his mouth, my love,
Ah! everything
we never got to say to one another?

This, then, is how the strutting Don Juan of 'Farewell' reacts when he finds out what it is actually like to lose a child.

Various critics have pointed out that in *Los versos del capitán* the frenzied eroticism of the *Veinte poemas* is tempered by a new-found sense of warmth and companionship. The poem 'No sólo el fuego' ('Not Only Fire') encapsulates this development:

Ay sí, recuerdo,
ay tus ojos cerrados
como llenos por dentro de luz negra,
todo tu cuerpo como una mano abierta,
como un racimo blanco de la luna,
y el éxtasis,

cuando nos mata un rayo,
cuando un puñal nos hiere en las raíces
y nos rompe una luz el cabello,
y cuando
vamos de nuevo
volviendo a la vida,
como si del océano saliéramos,
como si del naufragio
volviéramos heridos
entre las piedras y las algas rojas.

Pero hay otros recuerdos,
no sólo flores del incendio,
sino pequeños brotes
que aparecen de pronto
cuando voy en los trenes
o en las calles.

Te veo
lavando mis pañuelos,
colgando en la ventana
mis calcetines rotos
[. . .]
mujercita
de cada día.[9]

Ah yes, I remember,
ah your eyes closed
as if filled from within by black light,
your whole body like an open hand,
like one of the moon's white clusters,
and the ecstasy,
when a bolt of lightning strikes us down,

when a dagger cuts us to the quick
and light breaks our hair,
and when
we begin gradually
to come back to life,
as if emerging from the ocean,
as if returning wounded
from a shipwreck,
amongst stones and red seaweed.

But there are other memories,
not only flowers from the fire,
but little shoots which suddenly appear,
when I am on a train
or in the street.

I see you
washing my handkerchiefs,
hanging out my worn-out socks
at the window.
[...]
Little wife
of each and every day.

The Neanderthal sexism of these lines requires no comment.
They do, however, precisely sum up the two fundamental reasons
for Neruda's split with Delia. Firstly, as a consequence of an age
difference that had hardly seemed to matter in those first, heady
days in Madrid, their marriage had long been sexless. That may
not have been a pressing concern during their tense days in hiding,
but, now that he was free again, it was something that a man of
Neruda's appetites was never going to tolerate for long. Secondly,
whereas the cerebral, scatty Delia could hardly tell a fork from a

spoon, Matilde was a whizz in the kitchen. In short, in ditching one for the other Neruda was making that classic *machista* swap, leaving a woman who was his intellectual equal but a disaster round the house for a domestic goddess who rarely opened a book. Not a few of his more literary friends would disapprove.[10]

In June 1952, a month before the publication of *Los versos del capitán*, Neruda was informed that the warrant for his arrest had finally been withdrawn. At last, after more than three years in the wilderness, he could go home. When he arrived in Chile, however, the embittered González Videla, whose corrupt, six-year regime was rapidly crumbling, had a final surprise in store for him. He had personally paid for Maruca to come to Chile to file a lawsuit against Neruda for bigamy, since his divorce had been granted in Mexico, not Chile (where it was still illegal), and besides, Maruca had not been present to contest it. She and Neruda never met to negotiate, but in the end she accepted a relatively modest pay-off. We know little of her subsequent life, other than that she returned to Holland where she died in 1965, never having remarried.

Neruda would publish no more poetry until 1954, but juggling his marriage to Delia and his affair with Matilde kept him busy enough, not least since speculation concerning the intrigue behind *Los versos del capitán* was now rife. In December he and Delia attended the Second Writers' Congress in Moscow, but he managed to stagger their journeys home so that he could spend time with Matilde in Montevideo, only returning to Chile in January 1953. Two months later, on 5 March, the world learned of the death of Stalin. Neruda's personal response was a long, worshipful elegy-cum-panegyric, 'En su muerte' ('On His Death').[11] It makes for sickening reading, not just because of what we now know about Stalin's atrocities, but because it constitutes a dismal demonstration of Neruda's willingness to abandon every proper critical and aesthetic faculty when it came to flying the red flag. The rhetoric is boomingly hollow, the imagery shop-soiled and the message obscenely facile, besides not being particularly accurate (at the close, a poor Chilean fisherman reassures the grieving poet that Malenkov will now continue the good work, though things did not go quite so smoothly). Keats on Shelley or Auden on Yeats do not make for flattering comparisons. He also wrote an even more effusive prose obituary for *El Siglo*, which is worth quoting at length:

> The greatest of simple men, our master, has died. With his passing a heavy blow falls on knowledge and intelligence, on the culture of our glorious and stormy age. The greatest figure in contemporary philosophy has disappeared. But his passage through the realm of thought opened the doors of clarity and simplicity in the problems of our time and of times to come.
>
> In Stalin's shadow Science and Art, Poetry and Music burgeoned in the Soviet homeland with an immortal splendour. He left his creative imprint on man and wheat, on mountain and seed: he was the creator of peace in our time.[12]

With Matilde Urrutia (later his third wife) in 1952, the year in which he published *Los versos del capitán*, secretly dedicated to her.

Perhaps all one can say in Neruda's defence is that he was not alone; flick through the pages of many a leading Hispanic poet of the time (Alberti is a prime example) and you will find a litany of similarly chilling absurdities. Once more the toadying paid off, as in December 1953 Neruda was awarded the Stalin Peace Prize. Rather than distributing the money among his beloved *pueblo*, however, he preferred to spend it on a house for his lover. Situated at the foot of the Cerro San Cristóbal in Santiago's Bellavista district, this house, known as La Chascona, is now the home of the Pablo Neruda Foundation. One wonders what his illustrious benefactor, whom he had lauded as the very epitome of generosity, might have made of the decision.

In 1954 Neruda published two seemingly very different books. The first, *Las uvas y el viento* ('The Grapes and the Wind'), which contains the poem to Stalin, was composed between 1951 and 1953 and for the most part charts his journeys around the new Eastern European republics and the Far East (especially Maoist China), interleaving the loose narrative with love poems to Matilde, though often, as in certain pieces from *Los versos del capitán*, the personal and the political are conjoined. His most extreme experiment in what he imagined to be popular poetry, its crude ideology and desperately etiolated idiom are, to all intents and purposes, those of socialist realism. Neruda had an abiding affection for this woeful book, and took time out to defend it in his memoirs.[13] Nevertheless, with the possible exception of *Incitación al nixonicidio* (1973), his late diatribe against Nixon (which was very much a 'one off', a hurried response to the most pressing of circumstances) almost all critics view it as an embarrassing nadir in his output. The language and imagery are trite and repetitive and the message – that utopia lies just around the corner – offensively simplistic. Indeed, as Mario Vargas Llosa has pointed out with regard to committed literature in general, perhaps the chief weakness of the book is that its Manichean vision gives the reader nothing to ponder: either we swallow what the poet attempts to force-feed us or we keep our mouths firmly shut; there is none of that rich and challenging ambiguity that we find in the finest literary works.[14]

At this juncture it is also worth highlighting a shortcoming that intermittently compromises the other book Neruda published in 1954, as well as a great deal of his other purportedly popular verse: namely his ridiculously sanitized, caricatured and often condescending portrayal of the common people. These poems throng with unwaveringly honest, hard-working folk possessed of a natural wisdom who nevertheless remain nameless and face- less, cardboard cut-outs bereft of individual qualities, desires or, for that matter, failings (the idea that a builder or miner could do anything that did not entail heroic self-sacrifice was anathema to Neruda). Improbably, all that seems to interest them is tilling the earth and dreaming of a new socialist dawn. In short, what we get in *Las uvas y el viento* is not genuinely popular poetry (which deals more often and more entertainingly with ghosts, horse-trading, family feuds, adultery and the like, rather than tractors, collective farming and the dictatorship of the proletariat) but a distorted and potentially disabling intellectual version of it (one could never imagine Neruda's salt-of-the-earth farmers and fishermen wanting to do anything potentially more lucrative or fulfilling than till the land or cast their nets, provided they could do so in the right conditions; ambition and aspiration are dismissed as deplorable bourgeois vices). Like Tolstoy's Russian peasantry, Neruda's *pueblo* is primarily a figment of the poetic imagination.

The other book to which I have been referring is the first of four volumes of *Odas elementales*: he added two more in 1956 and 1957, while *Navegaciones y regresos* ('Voyages and Returns'; 1959) is effectively a fourth book of odes. At first glance it could hardly be more different than *La uvas y el viento*. The odes are supple, often delightfully breezy poems (line lengths tend to be very short, adding to the air of simplicity and spontaneity) which celebrate the least poetic of things, such as wood, potatoes, bread, socks and the poet's suit. Their tone is by turns whimsical, playful and affectionate, and many radiate a warmth and humour rarely found in his earlier work. Nevertheless, there is an agenda at work here every bit as rigid as the one that informs *Las uvas*, and this is swaggeringly set out in a preliminary poem, 'El hombre invisible' ('The Invisible Man'), which functions as a manifesto for the collection as a whole.[15] Here the speaker chides the poets of yore for their preening self-obsession, which may produce beautiful poetry but also causes them to turn their backs on those who toil, suffer and are the victims of social injustice. He, in contrast, will efface himself from his verse, altruistically allowing it to act as a conduit for the lives and labours of those routinely overlooked by poetry. This principle manifests itself as a schema or template in the poems themselves, and gives the supposed elementality of the objects, ideas and feelings treated a significant political twist, in so far as it is predicated on the restoration of a putatively pure, original use value that the rampant forces of capitalism have ruth-lessly commodified, with unfailingly disastrous consequences. The opening poem, 'Oda al aire' ('Ode to the Air'), provides a useful illustration. It takes the form of a conversation between the poet and the freewheeling breeze. The poet alerts the air to the dangers of venality; he has seen a price put on water and light, and the poor have gone thirsty and been forced to live – and die – in darkness. He does not want to see them asphyxiated too, so he begs the air to remain free and for the winds of change to blow so that:

> *Ya vendrá un día*
> *en que libertaremos*
> *la luz y el agua,*
> *la tierra, el hombre,*
> *y todo para todos*
> *será, como tú eres.*[16]

Soon a day will come
when we shall set free
light and water,
the earth, man,
and everything will be
for everyone,
just as you are.

It is noteworthy that these purportedly rousing climactic lines, which baldly summarize its political message, are by far the flattest and driest in the poem. Many of the other odes are marred by similar prosaic interjections or synopses.[17] As was the case in the *Canto general*, it is often the *least* political elements of the poems that are the most striking. Take, for example, Neruda's splendidly baroque description of the lowly onion.

Bajo la tierra
fue el milagro
y cuando apareció
tu torpe tallo verde
y nacieron
tus hojas como espadas en el huerto,
la tierra acumuló su poderío
mostrando tu desnuda transparencia,
y como en Afrodita el mar remoto
duplicó la magnolia
levantando sus senos,
la tierra
así te hizo,
cebolla.[18]

Beneath the earth
the miracle took place

and when your ungainly
green stem appeared
and your leaves emerged
like swords in the vegetable patch,
the earth hoarded its might,
displaying your naked transparency,
and just as the distant sea in Aphrodite,
duplicated the magnolia,
lifting up her breasts,
so the earth
made you,
onion.

The intended sense is clear: a simple onion, which will provide sustenance for the poor, is as lovely as the epitome of female beauty or the greatest work of bourgeois art (Boticelli surely comes to mind), and yet Neruda's own artistry in making this 'elementary' point is itself consummate. Indeed, counter to Neruda's own aesthetic exactions, it is tempting to see this strictly unnecessary though quite enchanting elaboration as a form of poetic surplus value to be enjoyed above and beyond the purely functional dimension of the poem. Surplus value is, of course, the very oil that lubricates the capitalist machine.

Nor is this the only factor that undercuts Neruda's 'naturalist' poetics and his emphasis on wholesome simplicity. Consider the title itself. The very notion of an 'elemental ode' is oxymoronic, since the ode is traditionally the loftiest of poetic utterances. Neruda's objective is clearly to bring poetry firmly down to earth, but by signalling that intention in this provocative way, he immediately opens up a debate *about* simplicity that is cultural to the core. Only a reader with a certain amount of literary-historical knowledge will get the point, and that presumably precludes the very folk whom Neruda elsewhere (see, for example, the first 'Oda

al libro' ['Ode to the Book'] and especially the 'Oda a la crítica'
['Ode to Criticism']) fiercely defends against the pernicious intru-
sions of the academe.[19] This omnipresent sense that simplicity and
popularity are notions to be reflected upon and explicated rather
than silently espoused means that few if any of the poems have a
genuinely popular, unselfconscious feel. Something similar might be
said regarding the poet's claim to invisibility. 'El hombre invisible'
must be about the most conspicuous disappearing act in literary
history. It is not simply that the poet has to be seen to disappear
that undermines his laudable premise ('Look, I'm gone!', he para-
doxically and insistently commands); it is that, after repeatedly
upbraiding fellow poets for 'always saying "I"', he himself proceeds
do so a full thirteen times in the second half of the poem (many
more, in fact, if one includes the 'I' implicit in the inflected first-
person verbs). Moreover, he indulges in precisely the same frivolous
activities (star-gazing, lazing around with his beloved) that other
poets irresponsibly prefer to the less palatable task of bearing
witness to the daily rough and tumble of life in the street. Perhaps
he feels his comradely credentials give him the right to do so, but
he never says so explicitly. Many of the subsequent poems take
the form of imagined or implied dialogues, often with hypothetical
detractors of his new poetics, so that they end up being more about
the poet's conception of and relationship to the common people
and its needs than the people themselves. As a consequence, he
is never completely hidden. Still, none of these shortcomings
and inconsistencies ultimately undermine the status of the *Odas
elementales* as one of Neruda's freshest and most original books.
Many of the odes are neither overtly political nor especially
elemental, at least in terms of their subject matter (which ranges
from the birds of Chile to Guatemala to César Vallejo, not a man
famed for his straightforwardness) and can be appreciated irrespective of the ideology to which in any case they do not and
perhaps cannot fully conform.[20]

The year 1954 also saw Neruda's fiftieth birthday. By now he was firmly established as Latin America's greatest living poet and, to celebrate the event, the University of Chile invited him to deliver a series of what proved to be highly revealing lectures. For the first time, Neruda spoke at length about his childhood and the profound influence of the southern Chilean landscape on his poetry.[21] It was also on this occasion that he told of the 'revelation' that he had experienced when addressing the workers of the Porters' Union back in 1938, which convinced him that 'the rhetoric and poetics of our age does not come from books. It comes from those heartrending encounters in which the poet comes face to face with his people for the first time.'[22] Yet while he was being honoured in public, Neruda's private life was as turbulent as ever. He was increasingly desperate to be with Matilde, while Delia was finally becoming suspicious. After returning from yet another senseless errand in March (this time Neruda had packed her off to Paris to see if she could persuade her former mentor, Fernand Léger, to illustrate a new edition of the *Canto general*), she broke down in tears during the reading of a love poem – manifestly not intended for her – from *Las uvas y el viento*. Soon afterwards, when rummaging through the poet's clothes in search of proof of his infidelity, she made the horrible discovery of a letter from Matilde in which the latter claimed to be pregnant for the third time. A distraught Delia immediately broke with Pablo and, despite his tears and sometimes dubious protestations (remarkably, he used the argument that Matilde had only done to Delia what Delia herself had done to Maruca back in Spain) she remained resolute. Indeed, although she remained in Chile for the rest of her life, she never saw her philandering former husband again. Their split had serious repercussions in Neruda's circle of acquaintances. Some, like Tomás Lago, were so appalled at his behaviour that they saw fit to end lifelong friendships. Neruda's mixture of underhandedness and spinelessness is certainly hard to stomach. Aside from anything else, he seems completely to have missed the point that it was *he* who was doing to Delia precisely what *he* had done to Maruca in Spain, choosing to ignore a difficult situation rather than address it and thereby inflicting far greater pain. Even those friends who stuck by Neruda were disappointed by what they considered to be a woeful lack of judgement on his part. Delia, refined, passionate and generous, was loved by all, whereas Matilde was seen as coarse and tacky. She was, however, a woman of steely determination, a formidable organizer and administrator who injected a significant dose of order into what remained a largely chaotic life. While she cooked, cleaned and managed a strict rota of visitors, Neruda could write at leisure. One might have expected Delia, alone again at seventy, to go to pieces, but nothing could have been further from the truth. Instead, she rediscovered her early passion for painting with a quite astonishing vigour, and went on to mount modest but successful exhibitions in both Europe and Latin America. Ironically, her favourite subject was horses, one of the most enduring symbols (of vitality, eros, untrammelled energy) in her former husband's poetry. She continued to paint for a further two decades and eventually died, aged one hundred and four, on 26 July 1989, having outlived every other character in this story.

Neruda was rattled by the fallout that followed his split from Delia, and consequently he and Matilde spent much of 1955 travelling outside Chile. They embarked on what would become a regular tour of the Soviet Union, China and the Eastern bloc republics, but also took in Brazil, Uruguay and Argentina on their return. However, just as the dust was beginning to settle on the domestic front, there occurred an outrage on an immeasurably greater scale that affected Neruda every bit as much as his break-up with Delia, and which was to cast a pall over his final years.

6

Crimes and Compromises

On 25 February 1956, in a speech delivered to the 20th Party Congress, President Nikita Khrushchev denounced Stalinism and the unspeakable crimes committed in its name. His revelations struck a terrible blow to communists the world over, and put prominent supporters of Stalin such as Neruda in an acutely uncomfortable position. Rumours of evil goings-on in Stalinist Russia had been spreading for years, with books such as Gide's *Retour de l'URSS*, Soviet dissident Victor Kravchenko's *I Chose Freedom* (1946) and, most recently, Richard Crossman's devastating compendium of essays, *The God that Failed* (1949), providing grim details of show trials, summary executions, forced collectivization and brutal labour camps. Closer to home, in 1951 Octavio Paz had published extracts from Nazi concentration camp survivor David Rossuet's anti-Stalinist writings in the Argentine cultural journal *Sur*. Hardliners like Neruda had become accustomed to dismissing such works as right-wing propaganda or arguing that, in order to create a totally new society, certain sacrifices, though regrettable, simply had to be made. The difference now, of course, was not simply the horrifying magnitude of those 'sacrifices', but the source from which the information regarding them emanated. Publicly, Neruda remained silent, but his poetry immediately began to betray signs of uncertainty and disillusionment. 'Oda al camino' ('Ode to the Road'), for example, from *Tercer libro de las odas* ('Third Book of Odes'; 1957), depicts a once confident traveller who has suddenly lost his way, and many other poems in the same volume are neither political nor optimistic in subject matter and tone.[1] As if to signal the rupture, Neruda dated many of these later pieces. In *Navegaciones y regresos*, meanwhile, a long, solemn ode marking the fortieth anniversary of the Russian revolution is dedicated not to Stalin but to Lenin, the founding father who made a pure 'pact with the earth'.[2] Still, this retreat into privacy hardly constituted a satisfactory response, at least for the poet's many detractors. That response, such as it was, was painfully slow in coming, and remained both evasive and incomplete. In an interview from 1971 he said, to an obviously sceptical questioner, that whilst the news had shocked him profoundly, he admired the Soviet Union for having had the courage and probity to make it public. When asked whether adherence to a utopian ideal meant that one could ultimately overlook the atrocities seemingly required to realize it, and which had caused the likes of Arthur Koestler to leave the Party, he dodged the question by claiming, with apparent seriousness, that he was not primarily interested in politics and that of the seven thousand or so pages of poetry that he had written, only three or four dealt with the subject. This outright lie would be laughable if it related to a matter any less grave.[3] In his memoirs he was marginally more forthcoming:

Many have believed me a diehard Stalinist . . . I am not particularly put out by this. Any judgement is possible in a diabolically confused era. The private tragedy for us Communists was to face the fact that, in several aspects of the Stalin problem, the enemy was right. This revelation, which was staggering, left us in a painful state of mind. Some felt that they had been deceived. Desperately, they accepted the enemy's reasoning and went over to its side. Others believed that the harrowing facts . . . proved the integrity of the Communist Party which survived, letting the world see the historical truth and accepting its own responsibility.

This has been my stand: above the darkness, unknown to me, of the Stalin era, Stalin rose before my eyes, a good-natured man of principles, as sober as a hermit, a titanic defender of the Russian Revolution. Moreover, this little man with his huge moustache had become a giant in wartime. With his name on its lips, the Red Army attacked and demolished the power of Hitler's demons.[4]

Even here one notes a reluctance to relinquish an outrageously idealized image of the young Stalin. However, the most important document detailing Neruda's reaction to and retrenchment in the wake of Khrushchev's revelations is the long, multipartite poem 'El episodio' ('The Episode') – note immediately the opaque, deliberately euphemistic title – included in the final section of *Memorial de Isla Negra*. The expression throughout is resolutely vague and the allusions oblique (Stalin is never mentioned by name, and an uninformed reader can gain no sense whatsoever of the extent and viciousness of his crimes) and the admission of any collective sense of responsibility fleeting and couched in figurative language that manages to be at once gaudily over-elaborate and offensively trite:

> *Y ya se sabe que nos desangramos*
> *cuando la estrella fue tergiversada*
> *por la luna sombría del eclipse.*[5]

> And it is well known that we bled
> when the star was overturned
> by the sombre moon of the eclipse.

Still, marshalling a host of his steeliest organic metaphors, he defiantly proclaims that the fight must go on:

> *Ahora veréis qué somos y pensamos.*
> *Ahora veréis qué somos y seremos.*

Somos la plata pura de la tierra,
el verdadero mineral del hombre,
encarnamos el mar que continúa;
la fortificación de la esperanza:
un minuto de sombra no nos ciega.[6]

Now you'll see who we are and what we think.
Now you'll see what we are and shall become.

We are the pure silver of the earth,
the mineral core of man,
we embody the endless motion of the sea;
the fortification of hope:
a single minute of shadow will not blind us.

That last formulation, casually reducing the torture and
murder of millions of innocent citizens to an unfortunate
blip, is truly remarkable. And yet that is clearly what Neruda
thought, as he immediately goes on to add that 'La historia se
apagó un minuto' ('History was switched off for a minute').[7]
Unlike fellow Latin American writers and intellectuals such as
Octavio Paz, Mario Vargas Llosa, and his countryman and friend
Jorge Edwards, all former socialists who later embraced liberal
democracy, Neruda seems never to have entertained the thought
that the communist dream might be essentially unworkable, the
source of rather than the panacea for the sort of evils and abuses
that he only partially confronted in 'El episodio'. What, in hindsight, are we to make of his unbending stance? In Neruda's defence,
we should not underestimate the role that personal experience
played in the formation of his political views: his first-hand encounter with fascism during the Spanish Civil War, his extensive
contact with the indigent of Chile and his political persecution
at the hands of a US-backed regime had all helped convince him

that fundamental change was necessary, and his instinctive if damagingly uncritical sense of social justice naturally pushed him towards communism. By the 1950s his global fame as a poet had made him a figurehead for the Left and a useful political pawn in the Cold War. The Soviet Union had been kind to him, and he felt a loyalty to the regime that made it difficult for him to speak out against it. Nevertheless, many others who had been in thrall to Stalin and whose novels, poems and paintings had long since been festooned with hammers and sickles *did* voice their dissent and publicly withdrew their allegiance. These included Neruda's friend, the Brazilian novelist and former communist hardliner Jorge Amado (1912–2001), who received a ticking off for his loss of faith in Neruda's memoirs. Still, even if we choose to comprehend Neruda's refusal to abandon the cause, we surely cannot forgive his strategic silences and disavowals in the face of subsequent acts of Soviet illiberalism or outright aggression. The first of these came as early as November of that same year, when Soviet forces entered Budapest to crush the anti-communist uprising. Neruda remained tight-lipped. Two years later, he uttered not a word of protest when the Soviet authorities banned the publication of *Doctor Zhivago* and prevented Boris Pasternak from travelling to Stockholm to receive the Nobel Prize. Indeed, despite mounting evidence, at no point did Neruda ever admit that writers or composers such as Shostakovich were persecuted or even restricted in the Soviet Union, angrily dismissing the charge as 'one more calumny of international reaction'.[8] As late as 1970, in one of his last major interviews, he stated without a whiff of irony that while disputes between writers and the state may exist, 'I have never seen less friction between a State and its writers than in socialist countries.'[9]

Away from the ideological fray, the travelling continued apace. In mid-1957 he and Matilde attended a Peace Congress in Ceylon. Neruda went in search of old acquaintances, but all he found was his former residence in the borough of Wellawatta, now overrun by creepers and marked for demolition. Accompanied by Jorge Amado and his wife, Zelia, the couple also stopped off in Rangoon. What he encountered was no longer the 'clean, luminous city' ruled over by the British that he had discovered in the 1920s but rather 'a half-deserted city, with shop windows almost completely empty and filth piled up in the streets', a ravaged, postcolonial ghost town.[10] There he attempted to track down Josie Bliss, only to find that entire neighbourhood where they had lived together had been destroyed. It was at that time, or shortly afterwards, that he wrote the doleful 'Regreso a una ciudad' and 'La desdichada' (see chapter Two). The opening lines of the latter stress the painful ineradicability of her memory:

La dejé en la puerta esperando
y me fui para no volver.

No supo que no volvería.

Pasó un perro, pasó una monja,
pasó una semana y un año.

Las lluvias borraron mis pasos
y creció el pasto en la calle,
y uno tras uno como piedras,
como lentas piedras, los años
cayeron sobre su cabeza.

Entonces la guerra llegó,
llegó como un volcán sangriento.
Murieron los niños, las casas.

Y aquella mujer no moría.[11]

I left her waiting at the door
and I departed never to return.

She never realized that I wouldn't come back.

A dog went by, a nun went by,
a week and a year went by.

The rains washed away my footprints
and grass grew in the street,
and one after another like stones,
like slow stones, the years
fell on her head.

Then came the war,
it came like a bloody volcano.
Children died, houses died.

But that woman wouldn't die.

'La desdichada' closes with a desolate picture of Josie still waiting, in vain, for her lover's return. From Rangoon the two couples proceeded to China. During their stay, an event occurred that dented Neruda's faith in a regime which until then he had supported uncritically. His friend, the poet Ai Qing, whom he viewed as an exemplary Party member, was sent into exile by Mao, who was then busy purging the country of undesirable supporters of the right. Just how deeply this affected the poet became clear in a speech delivered in Santiago some six years later, when Neruda, usually so reluctant to criticize 'the cause' in public, berated the Chinese authorities for their 'moral execution' of Qing, insisted that terror was anathema to a true communist and condemned Mao's domineering personality cult.[12]

After trips to Moscow, the Soviet republics of Abkhazia and Armenia, Paris, Finland and Sweden, he finally returned to Chile in December 1957, increasingly disenchanted but still unwilling to say so openly. Indeed, his next major book, *Estravagario*, is, on the face of it, one of the sunniest he ever wrote and positively overbrims with charm and good humour. The title itself, a conscious echo of the youthful *Crepusculario*, is a playful neologism, an amalgam of 'extravagante' ('extravagant' in all its senses, as it was written during a protracted period of travel) and 'estrafalario' ('bizarre'), and the book abounds with whimsy ('Por boca cerrada entran las moscas' ['Silence isn't Golden']), tongue-in-cheek philosophizing ('Y cuánto vive' ['And How Long Does a Man Live?']) and pure flights of fancy ('Fábula de la sirena y los borrachos' ['Fable of the Mermaid and the Drunks']).[13] It also contains some fine animal poems, such as the splendidly quirky 'Bestiario' ('Bestiary'), in which the poet casts himself as a would-be Dr Doolittle, trying to communicate with everything from fleas to frogs to penguins, and the beautiful 'Los caballos' ('Horses'), perhaps Neruda's finest evocation of an animal present everywhere in his poetry.[14] Much of *Estravagario*'s humour takes the form of self-mockery, perhaps the best example being 'Sobre mi mala educación' ('On My Bad Manners'), in which Neruda portrays himself as a hopeless mal-adroit.[15] However, this sidelining or undercutting of the poetic self also features in less frivolous poems, such as 'Partenogénesis' ('Parthenogenesis'), 'No me hagan caso' ('Just Ignore Me'), in which the poet begs to be left alone on his favourite stretch of shoreline, rummaging through the jetsam, or the witty but poignant 'Muchos somos' ('We Are Many').[16] As various critics have suggested, there is surely a political subtext to this restless self-questioning or out-right self-effacement. Devastated by the news of Stalin's crimes, he has lost that iron self-belief and missionary zeal that allowed him to proclaim himself his continent's chronicler in the *Canto general* or parade as the 'invisible man' of the *Odas elementales*. The false modesty of that collection is here superseded by a genuine, though also prudent, wish to stay out of the limelight. The corollary to this act of abdication is the conspicuous absence of politics in the book. Where history is mentioned, as in 'Pastoral' ('Pastoral'), it is as something from which the poet is seeking refuge.[17] Elsewhere, in the revealingly titled 'Cierto cansancio' ('A Certain Fatigue'), we find the first of a number of explicit rejections of the messianic cult of personality as a source of social retardation and collective brainwashing:

He visto algunos monumentos
erigidos a los titanes,
a los burros de la energía.
Allí los tienen sin moverse
con sus espadas en la mano
sobre sus tristes caballos.
Estoy cansado de las estatuas.
No puedo más con tanta piedra.

Si seguimos así llenando
con los inmóviles el mundo
cómo van a vivir los vivos?
[. . .]
Dejen tranquilos a los que nacen!
Dejen sitio para que vivan!
No les tengan todo pensado,
no les lean el mismo libro.[18]

I've seen various monuments
erected to titans,
to the donkeys of energy.
There they are, motionless,
sword in hand,

astride their sad horses.
I'm tired of statues.
I've had enough of all that stone.

If we carry on like this, filling
the world with immobile people,
how are the living going to live?
[. . .]
Leave those being born in peace!
Leave them some room in which to live!
Don't think all their thoughts for them,
Don't read to them all from the same book.

We could hardly be further away from the formulaic prescriptions of *Las uvas y el viento*.

Another initially baffling poem, 'No me pregunten' ('Don't Ask Me'), makes sense once we know the context: it turns out to be Neruda's first, characteristically elliptical, admission that he had been wrong to support Stalin, though – again typically – the latter is never mentioned. As in the later 'El episodio', his grotesquely upbeat recommendation is that the past simply be swept under the carpet in preparation for a new, more determined start.[19] Tellingly, on the rare occasions where social issues are addressed, they are stripped of all ideology. In 'El gran mantel' ('The Great Tablecloth'), for example, he laments the fact that so many in the world go hungry, but appeals to a vague sense of humanitarian justice rather than a five-year plan to solve the problem.[20] The abandoning of his grand historical mission leads to a new sense of fragility. If the revelation at Machu Picchu gave his individual life meaning by situating it within an evolving, collective continuum, now he begins to ponder his own mortality more sombrely, and poems such as 'Soliloquio en tinieblas' ('Soliloquy in the Dark'), 'Olvidado en otoño' ('Forgotten in Autumn') and 'Sueños de trenes' ('Dreams of Trains') betray an often stark sense of vulnerability.[21] In one of the book's finest pieces, 'Dónde estará la Guillermina?' ('Where Might Guillermina Be?'), he recalls being a blushing adolescent who instantly fell in love with one of his sister's friends and pauses to wonder what, after all these years, might have become of her.[22] This beautiful poem wistfully relumes what it simultaneously deems irrecoverable. It is also illustrative of a new tendency in Neruda's poetry that can be found elsewhere in *Estravagario* ('Sueños de trenes' and 'Carta para que me traigan madera' ['A Letter Asking for Wood'] are good examples) and which would culminate in *Memorial de Isla Negra*: the return to his childhood as a source of poetic inspiration.[23]

Estravagario, then, is one of Neruda's richest, most varied and – though not always in immediately obvious ways – most revealing books. Many, not least Robert Pring-Mill, have seen it as a key juncture in his *oeuvre*, which ushers in a more melancholy, 'autumnal' mode marked by meditative, often quasi-philosophical retrospection. This, as ever, is only part of the story. The year 1959 saw the publication of two more books, *Navegaciones y regresos*, which had been written in tandem with *Estravagario*, and *Cien sonetos de amor* ('One Hundred Love Sonnets'), a long and markedly uneven sonnet sequence for Matilde, which he had started back in 1957. That year also witnessed an epoch-making event that electrified Latin America and breathed new political life into the doubt-stricken poet: the Cuban Revolution. Here, it seemed, *was* a clean slate, a chance to put right what Stalin and his epigones had got so disastrously wrong. The enthusiasm and sense of hope that it ignited throughout a continent in the grip of a plethora of brutal, us-backed dictatorships (Trujillo in the Dominican Republic, Somoza in Nicaragua, Pérez Jiménez in Venezuela and so on) is almost impossible to convey in today's post-Cold War world, but back then it was almost palpable. Neruda, who had met Fidel Castro during a prolonged stay in Caracas early in 1959, promptly nailed his colours to the mast with the epic *Canción de gesta* ('Song of Protest'; 1960: the title refers to the medieval *chansons de geste*). He had begun to write it in 1958 as a protest against US political and economic intervention in Puerto Rico, but it soon became a hymn to the fledgling revolution. It was not, alas, destined to be well received in Cuba, and nor was its author. After yet more trips to the Soviet Union (where he formed part of the jury for the judiciously renamed Lenin Peace Prize) and Eastern Europe, and a lengthy sojourn in Paris, he and Matilde eventually headed for Cuba on 12 November 1960. It was to be a vexed visit, for a variety of reasons. Even though ideological sclerosis and authoritarianism were still a long way off, the carefree party atmosphere that Neruda, who had a lifelong knack of separating personal indulgence from collective political exigencies, had enjoyed during his previous visit in 1942 had all but vanished. Moreover, he was less than charmingly received by the legendary Che Guevara, who greeted Neruda at the National Bank slouched in a chair with his army boots resting on the desk. Ever the petit bourgeois when it came to social niceties, Neruda found this horribly uncouth although, given his political beliefs, he surely ought to have applauded the profanation. Then there was the irksome fact that in Cuba Neruda was, for once, not the centre of attention; that honour fell to fellow poet Nicolás Guillén who, to make matters worse, had made a pass at Matilde when they had travelled together through Romania back in 1951. Feinstein suggests that Neruda may also have been irritated by Fidel's early insistence that the revolution would not be governed by any single ideology, not even that of socialism.[24] Ironically, it was this initial guarantee of civil liberties, including those of artists and intellectuals, that proved so attractive to many of Fidel's supporters, and which began to wane only after he had declared the revolution socialist in the wake of the Bay of Pigs invasion of 1961. Neruda was also undoubtedly upset by the lukewarm response to *Canción de gesta*, which, as he was quick to point out, was the first book of poetry to be dedicated to the revolution. What caused this subdued reaction remains unclear, though one reason may be the inclusion of a poem addressed to Castro himself that seems to issue a veiled warning about the perilous seductions of autocracy:

> *Ésta es la copa, tómala, Fidel.*
> *Está llena de tantas esperanzas*
> *que al beberla sabrás que tu victoria*
> *es como el viejo vino de mi patria:*
> *no lo hace un hombre sino muchos hombres*
> *y no una uva sino muchas plantas:*
> *no una gota sino muchos ríos:*
> *no un capitán sino muchas batallas.*[25]

> This is the cup, take it, Fidel.
> It is full of so many hopes
> that when you drink from it you will know that your victory
> is like the vintage wine of my country:
> it is not made by one man but by many men
> and not by a single grape but by many vines:
> not by a single drop but by many rivers:
> not by a solitary captain but by many battles.

In the light of the depravities of those other conquering heroes, Stalin and Mao, this reads like no more than sage advice, though Fidel, supposedly offended by the implication, ultimately chose not to heed it. Given Neruda's resounding support for the Cuban cause (he ends *Canción de gesta* by affirming that with the advent of the revolution, 'History [any progressive, overarching sense of which was quietly abandoned in *Estravagario*] begins anew'), one can understand why he left the island piqued.[26]

The visit to Cuba was not Neruda's only unhappy experience in 1960. In May, his beloved south of Chile was devastated by a series of earthquakes. Thousands of lives were lost and tidal waves swept away much of the coastline, including Puerto Saavedra, that adolescent 'place of dreams' where he had written many of the *Veinte poemas de amor*. On hearing the terrible news, he composed the long, elegiac poem 'El cataclismo' ('The Cataclysm'), later included in *Cantos ceremoniales* ('Ceremonial Chants'), published the following year. This often melancholy volume, made up of ten long poems, was one of two books that Neruda published in 1961. The other was *Piedras de Chile* ('Stones of Chile'), a sort of geological colophon to the 'Canto general de Chile' that is also a hymn to Isla Negra and the surrounding coast. Here we find Neruda at his most chthonic, delving into the hiddenmost strata of the earth in search of purity and permanence. The most important publishing event of the year, however, was the appearance of a commemorative edition of the *Veinte poemas de amor* to mark the sale of the millionth copy. Published by Losada of Buenos Aires, it featured a specially commissioned prologue by the author that offered tantalizing glimpses into the circumstances of its composition. By now it had become the definitive Latin American *Ars Amatoria*, and its verses were being declaimed, whispered or panted at every moment of the day and night somewhere on the continent. As Chilean novelist and playwright Ariel Dorfman ruefully notes, such popularity had its drawbacks. When, aged fourteen, he dared to murmur the famous opening line of Poem 20 ('Tonight I can write the saddest lines') into the ear of an older girl, she turned on him, saying, 'Neruda! You're the fifth half-baked poet who's recited that to me this month. Can't you try something else?'[27] Still, the whispering and panting must still be going on, since at the time of writing the book has sold an astounding eight million copies. After the relentless peregrinations of the previous years, 1961 proved relatively tranquil, as did 1962, though the latter began with an important literary undertaking. In January, picking up a strand of his work initially fleshed out in 'Yo soy' and later developed in parts of *Estravagario*, Neruda began to compose a series of twelve revealing autobiographical pieces for the Brazilian journal *O Cruzeiro Internacional*. Published under the title 'Memorias y recuerdos de Pablo Neruda: Las vidas del poeta' ('Memoirs and Recollections of Pablo Neruda: The Poet's Lives'), they would later be incorporated, with only minimal alterations, into his memoirs. Needless to say, later that year another book of poetry appeared. Titled *Plenos poderes* ('Fully Empowered') it opens with a poem which, perhaps better than any other, sums up Neruda's hastily revised, much more modest conception of his métier at that time. 'Deber del poeta' ('The Poet's Duty') reads like a chastened reprise of the cocksure 'El hombre invisible':

> *A quien no escucha el mar en este viernes*
> *por la mañana, a quien adentro de algo,*
> *casa, oficina, fábrica o mujer,*
> *o calle o mina o seco calabozo:*
> *a éste yo acudo y sin hablar ni ver*
> *llego y abro la puerta del encierro*
> *y un sin fin se oye vago en la insistencia,*
> *un largo trueno roto se encadena*
> *al peso del planeta y de la espuma,*
> *surgen los ríos roncos del océano,*
> *vibra veloz en su rosal la estrella,*
> *y el mar palpita, muere y continúa.*[28]

To whoever cannot hear the sea
this Friday morning, to whoever is cooped up
in house, office, factory or woman,
or street or mine or waterless cell:
to him I go and without speaking or seeing

I arrive and open the door of his prison
and something vague, endless, insistent is heard,
a long, broken rumble of thunder chains itself
to the mass of the planet and the foam,
the groaning rivers of the ocean rise,
a fleeting star throbs in its rose bed
and the sea heaves, dies and endures.

Instead of offering the oppressed grand but insubstantial Utopian
dreams, he supplies them with a breath of sea air as welcome
relief from their daily toil. Note too that here he finally pulls off
his promised vanishing act, since after the words 'I open the door
of his prison' the poetic voice melts into the background and the
sounds and swell of the ocean (conveyed via a long series of sibi-
lances, alliterations and pounding rhythms) come flooding in.
This, then, is the poet's duty: to provide, by channelling the wild
ocean into the 'taza eterna' ('eternal cup') of his poem, solace for
the 'corazón oscuro' ('sombre heart') of the oppressed.[29] This hardly
amounts to a political philosophy, but the poem is all the better
for it. *Plenos poderes* also contains several quietly philosophical
compositions, especially 'La palabra' ('The Word'), 'Los nacimientos' ('Births') and 'Pasado' ('Past'), as well as further poems
that revisit the world of Neruda's childhood.[30] The finest of these
is 'Regresó el caminante' ('The Wanderer Has Returned'), written
after a trip to Temuco during which the poet realized that the
rustic outpost of his childhood had been completely subsumed
by the modern city, and that if that distant idyll was to survive it
must do so in his verse.[31] That experience provided one of the seeds
that would later blossom into the fully autobiographical *Memorial
de Isla Negra*. The only overtly political poem in the collection, 'El
pueblo' ('The People'), is one of his most moving, despite the rather
hackneyed exhortations that creep in towards the end. Rather than
a diatribe it is part lament, part hymn of praise, and the tone is not

hectoring but humbly respectful. In it, Neruda remembers all those toiling men and women whom affluent society has exploited and swiftly forgotten, even as it enjoys the fruits of their labours. It is the worker, not the poet, who is the real invisible man, though for all the wrong reasons:

> *Era el hombre sin duda, sin herencia,*
> *sin vaca, sin bandera,*
> *y no se distinguía entre los otros,*
> *los otros que eran él,*
> *desde arriba era gris como el subsuelo,*
> *como el cuero era pardo,*
> *era amarillo cosechando el trigo,*
> *era negro debajo de la mina,*
> *era color de piedra en el castillo,*
> *en el barco pesquero era color de atún*
> *y color de caballo en la pradera:*
> *cómo podía nadie distinguirlo*
> *si era el inseparable, el elemento,*
> *tierra, carbón o mar vestido de hombre?*[32]

> That was the man all right, without inheritance,
> no cow, no coat of arms,
> and indistinguishable from the rest,
> from the others who were himself,
> from above he was grey, like clay,
> he was brown, like leather,
> he was yellow when harvesting wheat,
> he was black when down in the mine,
> he was stone-coloured in the castle,
> in the fishing boat he was the colour of tuna,
> and horse-coloured in the meadows:
> how could anyone make him out

if he had no being of his own, was base matter,
earth, coal or sea in a man's clothing?

The answer to this final question is the poem itself, which renders visible what for so long has been shamefully overlooked. Comparing this measured, sensitive, often solemn poem with the obstreperous, rabble-rousing 'El pueblo victorioso' from *Canto general* reveals what is almost a sea-change in the poet's attitude to his subject. From a political point of view, this is most evident in his treatment of proletarian workers, whom he now portrays as a gathering of discrete, finite individuals rather than the disembodied 'collective subject' of Marxist history.

Throughout 1963 there was much talk of Neruda being awarded the following year's Nobel Prize. Given what, publicly at least, remained his extreme political position, he was always going to be a controversial candidate, so it is hardly surprising that an aggressive smear campaign against him was rapidly organized. Backed by the CIA, which kept files on the poet, its public front was the Congress for Cultural Freedom, founded in West Berlin in 1950, which violently opposed communism in all its manifestations. Prominent members included Karl Jaspers, Bertrand Russell, Benedetto Croce, Arthur Koestler, Tennessee Williams and Robert Lowell. The Congress commissioned a privately circulated 'report', compiled by French writer and editor René Tavernier, which accused Neruda of being a Soviet stooge whose poetry was no more than incendiary leftist propaganda. Neruda did not receive the Nobel Prize in 1964, though it is difficult to gauge how far Tavernier's report may have affected the decision, since it was eventually awarded to fellow communist Jean-Paul Sartre, who promptly refused to accept it.

Between 1962 and 1964 Neruda had been busy putting together a book expressly intended as a sixtieth birthday present to himself. Its working title was *Sumario* ('Summary'), but he eventually called it *Memorial de Isla Negra*. Taking the form of a synoptic verse autobiography, it is a lengthy stocktaking of one of the most dramatic and controversial literary lives of the twentieth century, though one that, it turned out, was far from over. In a curious mirroring of the *Canto general*, an initially clear sense of chronology gradually unravels as the book progresses and eventually breaks down altogether. The opening section, 'Donde nace la lluvia' ('Where the Rain is Born'), takes us from Neruda's childhood in Temuco to his arrival in Santiago, and includes touching poems about the mother he never knew ('Nacimiento' ['Birth']), his father ('El padre' ['The Father']) and stepmother ('La mamadre' ['My Other Mummy']), as well as his schooldays ('El colegio en invierno' ['School in Winter']), his first sexual experiences ('El sexo' ['Sex']) and the southern climes that left an indelible imprint on his poetry ('El primer mar' ['First Encounter with the Sea'], 'La tierra austral' ['Southern Land'] and 'El lago de los cisnes' ['Swan Lake']).[33] Intriguingly, when attempting to recall how and when he began to think of himself as a poet, it is the vertiginous, disquietingly erotic experience of staring at the heavens, the same experience that led him to write *El hondero entusiasta*, that he evokes:

> *Vi de pronto*
> *el cielo*
> *desgranado*
> *y abierto,*
> *planetas,*
> *plantaciones palpitantes,*
> *la sombra perforada,*
> *acribillada*
> *por flechas, fuego y flores,*
> *la noche arrolladora, el universo.*
>
> *Y yo, mínimo ser,*
> *ebrio del gran vacío*

constelado,
a semejanza, a imagen
del misterio,
me sentí parte pura
del abismo,
rodé con las estrellas,
mi corazón se desató en el viento.[34]

Suddenly I saw
the heavens
unfastened
and open,
planets,
throbbing plantations,
the darkness perforated,
riddled
with arrows, fire and flowers,
the overpowering night, the universe.

And I, a minuscule being,
drunk with the great, star-filled void,
the image and likeness
of mystery,
felt myself a pure part
of the abyss,
I wheeled with the stars,
my heart was unleashed in the wind.

Despite his increasingly functionalist, pragmatic view of literature,
this conviction that there is something awe-inspiringly cosmic at
the heart of *poesis* remains profoundly Romantic. Also of note here
is the channelling of the lithe, sinuous verse form developed in the
Odas elementales towards new and quite different ends. On this

occasion the brief, darting lines are intended to reproduce the young Neruda's breathless wonder before the magnitude of the heavens. Despite his advancing years, Neruda hated to repeat himself, and tirelessly redeployed the tools of his now formidable poetic armoury or, when necessary, forged new ones.

The next section, 'La luna en el laberinto' ('The Moon in the Labyrinth') takes us from Neruda's carefree days in Santiago to his years in the Far East. Highlights include two pairs of poems to the now distant loves of his youth, Teresa and Albertina ('Amores: Terusa/Rosaura (i + ii)' ['Loves: Terusa/Rosaura (i + ii)']), character sketches of various 'mad friends' from his early drinking days and 'El opio en el Este' ('Opium in the East'), a haunting recollection of the experience of smoking opium, which counterpoises a Baudelairean evocation of the deliciously weightless, disembodied state that the drug induces with a social critique of the wretchedness of the lives of those who depended on it.[35] By the time we get to 'El fuego cruel' ('The Cruel Fire'), the narrative begins to go awry. It opens with memories of the Spanish Civil War and his return to Chile as a changed man ('Tal vez cambié desde entonces' ['Perhaps from that Moment I Changed']).[36] Later poems, such as 'En las minas de arriba' ('Way Up There in the Mines') and 'Revoluciones' ('Revolutions') deal with his increasing involvement with popular politics and his developing view of the poet's mission, but others, like 'Soliloquio en las olas' ('Soliloquy Amidst the Waves'), 'Cordilleras de Chile' ('Mountain Ranges of Chile'), 'Me siento triste' ('I Feel Sad') or 'El mar' ('The Sea') are no more than contemplative asides, albeit sometimes very beautiful ones.[37] Unexpectedly, he then returns to his time in Burma and Ceylon, and this reversion yields the two heartrending poems about Josie Bliss (see chapter Two). The section then peters out with a rather disjointed series of poems detailing various, often unrelated experiences from his years in exile. Section 4, 'El cazador de raíces' ('The Hunter after Roots') is at once the most incongruous and the most absorbing. Much of it revolves around an urgent quest for origins in the hidden substrata of nature (which, as always, is the nature of southern Chile) that clearly recalls the first five sections of 'Alturas de Macchu Picchu' or indeed earlier poems such as 'Naciendo en los bosques' ('Being Born in the Woods') from *Tercera residencia*, one of Neruda's first significant attempts to banish the pessimism of his early verse by seeking solace in the self-renewing natural world.[38] One of the poems, 'Lo que nace conmigo' ('What is Born with Me'), reads like a revisionist take on 'Galope muerto', the language and syntax of which it seems consciously to mimic. Now, however, the emphasis is firmly on birth rather than death:

Como un tambor eterno
suenan las sucesiones, el transcurso
de ser a ser, y nazco, nazco, nazco
con lo que está naciendo, estoy unido
al crecimiento, al sordo alrededor
de cuanto me rodea, pululando,
propagándose en densas humedades,
en estambres, en tigres, en jaleas.
Yo pertenezco a la fecundidad
Y creceré mientras crecen las vidas.[39]

Like an eternal drum
the cycle of successions sounds, the passage
from being to being, and I'm born, I'm born, I'm born
with what is coming into being, I am one
with growing, with the mute surround
of everything that encircles me, teeming,
propagating itself in dense waves of moisture,
in stamens, in tigers, in jellies.
I belong to fruitfulness
and I'll grow as long as lives keep growing.

With Guatemalan novelist and Nobel laureate Miguel Ángel Asturias, 1965. Neruda had used Asturias' passport to escape to Europe in 1949.

No longer is the poet overwhelmed by a 'desorden vasto' ('vast disorder') that surrounds him in a dizzying 'rodeo constante' ('constant wheeling') and which his 'corazón palido no puede abarcar' ('pale heart cannot grasp'); instead, he feels like an integral part of a dynamic organic process.[40] Perhaps fittingly, this section also contains the only two poems that Neruda ever explicitly addressed to Delia del Carril ('Amores Delia (i + ii)' ['Loves Delia i + ii']).[41] I say 'fittingly' with a due sense of irony, since Delia, to whom the poet would always give his first drafts for comment, was sternly critical of Neruda's sometimes incontinent organicism, which, she pointed out, manifested itself in the gross overuse of one particular word: 'raíces' ('roots'). Any lingering pretence of narrative continuity disappears with the inclusion of the wonderful 'Serenata de Mexico', a reminder of the crucial role his Mexican experiences played in transforming him from a 'padre del llanto' ('father of weeping') into a man at home in the world and intensely aware of his American identity. The closing section, 'Sonata crítica' ('Critical Sonata'), is largely taken up with 'El episodio' and other poems that cautiously set out his ideological reorientation. By far

Receiving his honorary doctorate in Oxford, 1965.

the most revealing of these is 'La verdad' ('The Truth'), in which he rejects all forms of dogmatism, whether aesthetic (socialist realism, which he now mocks) or political (Stalinism, though as usual it is never mentioned), asking of the 'truth', 'No te detengas tanto/que te endurezcas en la mentira' ('Don't stand still for so long/that you harden into lies'), in an obvious allusion to the deleterious bureaucratization of fundamental revolutionary energies under Stalin. In accordance with this hastily rediscovered spirit of pluralism, he ends by refusing to be prescriptive when it comes to ideological matters:

> *No soy rector de nada, no dirijo,*
> *y por eso atesoro*
> *las equivocaciones de mi canto.*[42]

> I'm no director, I don't give orders,
> and that's why I treasure
> the errors of my song.

The far from invisible evangelist of the *Odas elementales* is now well and truly out of sight. The book's final poem, 'El futuro es espacio' ('The Future is Space'), is a correspondingly vague – some might say vapid – statement of belief in an unshackled future, though one in which hammers and sickles are conspicuous by their absence. *Memorial de Isla Negra* was to be the last book of poetry that Neruda composed on such an ambitious scale. Whilst, like earlier works such as *Tentativa del hombre infinto* and *Canto general*, it fails to cohere into a truly satisfying whole, the level of inspiration and execution is consistently high and, not for the first time, only dips significantly when he indulges in the polemicizing and dubious self-justification of poems such as 'El episodio'.

The year 1965 involved yet more intense travelling, including trips to France, Hungary, Yugoslavia, Finland and the Soviet Union,

With Arthur Miller and Uruguayan critic Emir Rodríguez Monegal at a meeting of the International PEN Club in New York, 1966.

where he saw the Lenin Peace Prize awarded to his old friend Rafael Alberti. In June Neruda also made his first visit to Britain, where, thanks to the dynamism of Robert Pring-Mill, he became the first Latin American to receive an honorary doctorate from the University of Oxford. During his stay in Hungary he met up with his friend and one-time photo-double Miguel Ángel Asturias, with whom he embarked on a month-long gastronomic tour, the fruits of which were another bout of phlebitis and a co-authored glutton's handbook titled simply *Comiendo en Hungría* ('Eating in Hungary'). Like many a stern socialist proselytizer, Neruda saw no discrepancy between leading a life of riotous excess himself and recommending one of dignified frugality for the labouring masses, who would have to make do with onions, tomatoes and the odd artichoke (all praised in the *Odas elementales*) while he gorged on venison and foie gras (to which he composed a poem), washed down with litres of tokay and Bull's Blood (which inspired sufficient enthusiasm to merit a sonnet).[43] In Yugoslavia, mean-while, he attended the thirty-third congress of the International PEN Club in Bled. There Arthur Miller invited him to participate in the following year's gathering in New York, where Neruda was, of course, *persona non grata*. He could scarcely have imagined, however, the quarter from which opposition to his visit would eventually come.

7

A Cuban Missile

The early months of 1966 were spent negotiating the terms of
Neruda's divorce from Delia. It was a delicate and painful process,
but an initially intransigent Delia eventually gave way and the
divorce was granted on 16 June. Immediately afterwards, Neruda
set off for New York. His presence there at the height of the Cold
War was always going to cause ructions; indeed, Miller virtually
had to beg the US Foreign Office to let him enter the country, since
communists were officially banned. He was soon making waves,
noisily condemning the Vietnam War at every available opportunity
and getting caught up in ideological skirmishes with liberal writers
such as Ignazio Silone, another prominent member of the Congress
for Cultural Freedom, about the plight of creative artists under
totalitarian regimes, especially in the Soviet Union. Still, Neruda
enjoyed his stay immensely and the congress was a great success.
Latin America, which was then experiencing a continent-wide
flourishing in arts and letters (especially the novel, which was
enjoying what has since become known as the 'Boom'), was strongly
represented, with Mexican novelist Carlos Fuentes, Vargas Llosa,
Nicanor Parra and Brazilian 'concrete' poet Haroldo de Campos all
participating. On their way back to Chile, Pablo and Matilde made
stops in Mexico and Peru, where, in an august public ceremony,
president Fernando Belaúnde Terry awarded Neruda the Orden
del Sol del Perú for 'Alturas de Macchu Picchu'. At the time it must
have seemed like an eminently satisfying conclusion to his travels,

but it was not to prove so for, shortly after his arrival, he was delivered a bombshell from the least expected of sources: Cuba. Unsurprisingly, the Cubans had elected to boycott the New York conference, and now publicly rebuked 'comrade' Neruda for not having followed suit. On 31 July the official Communist Party newspaper, *Granma*, published a long open letter, signed by more than a hundred Cuban writers and intellectuals, accusing Neruda, by willingly setting foot in enemy territory, of providing the US with vital ammunition in its anti-communist crusade. The reproach extended to his acceptance of the award from Belaúnde Terry, whose government opposed Castro's regime. How would Neruda have liked it, they asked, had he been forced to watch a fellow Latin American writer receive such an honour from González Videla while he was on the run? Whilst, as Hernán Loyola claims, the letter as a whole may have been both unjust and unjustified, the latter point at least is not entirely unwarranted, since Neruda, as we know, could be merciless in his condemnation of writers who supported political causes that were not to his liking. The driving force behind the attack was almost certainly Castro himself, who was clearly still riled by those anodyne lines from *Canción de gesta* cited in the previous chapter. Neruda fired back a cable reaffirming his 'passionate adhesion' to the Cuban cause and arguing that he had gone to the States not as a sign of his tacit approval for US foreign policy but rather to promote and defend socialist ideas there. Still, the damage – and it was to be profound and lasting damage – was done and, despite receiving several invitations, Neruda would never set foot in Cuba again. His parting shot in the whole sorry business – a prime example of the sort of childish, internecine bickering that has so often hampered the Latin American Left – was the addition of a new poem, 'Juicio Final' ('Last Judgement'), to later editions of *Canción de gesta*. In it he derides the co-signatories of the letter, singling out Nicolás Guillén, novelist Alejo Carpentier (1904–1980) and poet and essayist Roberto Fernández Retamar (*b.* 1930) for especial censure, and ends by saying that, his conscience clear, he will continue to support a revolution that will long outlive a 'dead insult'.[1]

At least the year ended on a happy note. On 28 October he married Matilde at Isla Negra, and days later *Arte de pájaros* ('The Art of Birds') appeared. A sort of spoof ornithological encyclopedia (several of the birds featured, including the splendidly silly 'Tonti-vuelo', are Neruda's inventions), it is by Neruda's standards an occasional book, but a charming and often funny one, full of the sorts of punning, nonce words and absurdist humour that were features of *Estravagario*. Birds are invariably a positive presence in Neruda's verse, connoting grace, elegance and vibrancy, as well as suggesting the flights of the poetic imagination. That particular association is evident as early as the *Veinte poemas de amor*, where he refers to the act of creation as akin to that of 'releasing birds'.[2] Years later, he joked that it was the poet's prime duty to 'pajarear' (literally 'to bird about/around', though it also means 'to loaf around' or, in the Southern Cone, 'to have one's head in the clouds'), by which he clearly meant to spread feelings of joy and vitality among his readership.[3]

The year 1967 ushered in a new round of travels, which must have taken their toll on the increasingly ailing poet, as recurring attacks of phlebitis and gout – that quintessentially patrician malady, about which he would moan because it stopped him from eating caviar – meant that he often had difficulty walking.[4] These included the annual jaunt in Moscow to attend the Soviet Writers' Conference in May. On a further trip to London in August, to participate in the Poetry International Conference, there took place an embarrassingly stagy 'reconciliation' with Octavio Paz, though, predictably, Neruda makes no mention of it in his memoirs. Paz, however, proved more generous. Whilst he never wavered in his condemnation of what he saw as Neruda's dogmatic and often duplicitous politicking, he was later happy to declare his 'dearest enemy' the greatest Hispanic poet of his generation, going as far as to describe their awkward reunion as 'one of the best things that has happened to me: rekindling my friendship with a man I loved and admired'.[5]

Neruda's most intriguing trip that year, however, was a lightning visit to Spain, his first since the Civil War. On 16 April the Catalan author and publisher Esther Tusquets met Neruda in Barcelona, where the poet proceeded to take her on a nostalgic tour of the city in which he had last set foot in 1937. According to Feinstein, it was on this 'secret stop-off', about which Tusquets supposedly remained tight-lipped, that he met Gabriel García Márquez who, years later, fictionalized the encounter in his story 'Me alquilo para soñar' ('I Sell My Dreams'), in which Neruda is depicted by the narrator as the latterday embodiment of a 'refined, gluttonous Renaissance Pope'.[6] The description, though hardly flattering, is by no means inaccurate. However, as Tusquets herself revealed in a newspaper article in 2004, the visit was entirely legal (like the other passengers, Neruda was allowed to use a landing pass rather than a passport to go ashore) and during the few hours of its duration he met just three people, none of whom was García Márquez, who only moved there in late 1967.[7] Neruda would visit the city again in June 1970 and it was on that occasion that the Colombian writer based his story. Despite the hectic schedule, books continued to appear at a bewildering rate. *La barcarola* ('Barcarolle') is at once an ecstatic love song to Matilde and a virtuoso experiment in versification in honour of Rubén Darío, whose centenary fell that year. The title may allude indirectly to the opening poem of the latter's *Cantos de vida y esperanza* (1905), in which Darío casts himself in the role of amorous gondolier:

El dueño fui de mi jardín de sueño
Lleno de rosas y cisnes vagos;
El dueño de las tórtolas, el dueño
De góndolas y liras en los lagos.[8]

I was the master of my garden of dreams
full of roses and errant swans;
the master of turtle doves, the master
of gondolas and lyres on lakes.

The flow of the *barcarolle* is periodically and at times jarringly
interrupted by eleven intercalated 'episodes', many of which (such
as 'Las campanas de Rusia' ['The Bells of Russia'] or 'Lord Cochrane
de Chile', a late footnote to 'Los Libertadores' from the *Canto general*)
deal with completely extraneous socio-historical material, though one,
an oddly lacklustre effort, is dedicated to Darío himself. Perhaps
Neruda was attempting to reproduce the private/public counter-
point of books such as *Los versos del capitán* or *Las uvas y el viento*,
though here the interweaving seems forced. One of these episodes,
'Fulgor y Muerte de Joaquín Murieta' ('Splendour and Death of
Joaquín Murieta'), which deals with the adventures and tribulations
of a legendary Chilean bandit during the Californian gold rush
of the 1850s, is of particular interest, since it formed the basis for
Neruda's first and only theatrical work of the same title, which
was premiered in October of that year. Even the poet's staunchest
admirers concede that, despite boasting a number of beautiful
passages, most of which are declaimed by a chorus that comments
on the action in the manner of a Greek tragedy, from a purely
dramatic point of view the work is deeply flawed. It fails persuasively
to combine satirical and tragic elements, is populated by paper-thin
caricatures rather than fully formed characters and, bizarrely,
Murieta himself does not appear until after his execution, when his
severed head addresses the audience in a misjudged attempt at a
coup de théâtre. Packed with songs, chants and popular refrains, it
offers more promising material for an oratorio or opera than for a
work of conventional theatre. Indeed, in 1998 Chilean composer
Sergio Ortega set it to music, although it is ill served by the soupy
romantic pastiche and tackily orchestrated folk tunes of the score.

The following year proved more tranquil, at least as far as travelling was concerned. In May Neruda was made a member of the North American Academy of Arts and Letters. His letter of thanks makes for startling reading. In it, he acknowledges the lofty honour of having his 'meagre *oeuvre*' deemed worthy to stand alongside that of 'such luminaries' as André Gide and T. S. Eliot![9] Gide, as we know, was one of the principal targets of Neruda's initial attacks on vapid aestheticism, and not so many years earlier he had contemptuously dismissed Eliot as a 'false, reactionary mystic'.[10] Prestigious awards, of course, have a habit of inducing amnesia in their recipients. In July Losada brought out a third, greatly expanded two-volume edition of his *Complete Works* (previous editions had appeared in 1957 and 1962), but Neruda had hardly had time to enjoy the accompanying accolades when international politics reared its ugly head again. In August Warsaw Pact troops poured into Czechoslovakia, putting a brutal end to the 'Prague Spring' and Alexander Dubcek's democratizing reforms. Once again, to his immense shame, Neruda uttered not a word of protest, either in public or in private, though his feelings about world politics at the time can in part be gauged from his next book, *Las manos del día* ('The Hands of the Day'), which appeared in early November. Throughout its pages he repeatedly expresses his sense of guilt at never having crafted anything useful with his own hands, and it suddenly dawns on him, despite what he had always claimed, that the act of writing poetry, even the most heartfelt, generous poetry, is not equivalent to those of tilling the land, baking, chopping wood or putting food on the table; one simply cannot, *pace* Seamus Heaney, dig with one's pen, and writing about the dilemma does nothing to remedy it:

> *Cuándo me vio nunguno*
> *cortando tallos, aventando el trigo?*
> *Quién soy, si no hice nada?*

Cualquiera, hijo de Juan,
tocó el terreno
y dejó caer algo
que entró como la llave
entra en la cerradura
y la tierra se abre de par en par.
[...]
La agricultura nunca se ocupó de mis libros.[11]

When did anyone see me
cutting stalks,
winnowing wheat?
Who am I, if I have never done anything?
Anyone, some son of Juan,
touched the earth
and dropped something
which entered as a key
enters a lock
and the earth opens wide.
[...]
Agriculture never concerned itself with my books.

The humblest worker, it seems, achieves more by sowing a handful
of seed than Neruda had in composing his entire *oeuvre*. That last
line in particular reads like a gloomy palinode to the close of the
second 'Oda al libro', where the poet triumphantly portrays nature
and culture wedded in the image of 'el campesino/arando/con
un libro' ('the peasant/ploughing/with a book').[12] Feinstein takes
Neruda to task over *Las manos del día*, dismissing it as a mawkish
and insincere 'guilt trip'.[13] This is somewhat harsh. For the previous
twelve years at least, Neruda's once fervent belief that a new socialist
age was about to dawn had taken a terrible battering. He had
watched the US pursue an ever more aggressive anti-communist

policy abroad and seen the Left disastrously discredited by its own, often monstrous forms of authoritarianism. Aging, increasingly frail, and faced with a world seemingly bent on self-destruction, it is no wonder that his labours as a poet must at times have seemed futile. As the bombs rained down on Vietnam, his rhetorical question regarding that putative new era ('It did seem that it was dawning, didn't it?') is more pitiful than disingenuous.[14] It seems highly significant, then, that right at the heart of *Las manos del día* the poet, who had earlier berated himself as a star-gazing 'child of the moon', should suddenly turn his back on the ugliness of the world and seek succour in the bosom of night, just as he had done during his youth:

> *Amamántame,*
> *noche,*
> *déjame sacudir,*
> *vaciar el líquido*
> *de tus ubres nocturnas,*
> *húndeme en tu regazo*
> *horizontal, entre las poblaciones*
> *de tu maternidad, por las moradas*
> *de tus frías antorchas.*[15]

> Suckle me,
> night,
> let me shake,
> empty the liquid
> from your nocturnal teats,
> bury me in your horizontal lap,
> amidst your teeming
> maternity, amongst the dwellings
> of your cold torches.

This impassioned plea bears a striking resemblance to a passage from *Tentativa del hombre infinito*, penned over forty years earlier:

oh noche huracán muerto resbala tu oscura lava
mis alegrías muerden tus tintas
mi alegre canto de hombre chupa tus duras mamas[16]

oh night dead hurricane your dark lava slides
my joys bite your shades
my joyous, manly song sucks on your hard breasts

Such seeking of refuge in a nature suffused with idealized childhood memories is a feature of much of Neruda's late verse. Indeed, it figures prominently in his next major book, *Fin de mundo* ('World's End'; 1969), in poems such as the wonderful 'El estrellero' ('The Astrologer'), 'El tardío' ('The Late One'), 'Fundaciones' ('Foundations'), 'Canción con paisaje y río' ('Song with Landscape and River') and 'Anduve' ('I Walked'), which ends with a soulful entreaty – 'Oh antigua lluvia, ven y sálvame/de esta congoja inamovible' ('Oh rain of old, come save me/from this unrelenting anguish') – that distantly recalls the close of 'Vuelve el otoño', written in Spain back in 1935, in which the Chile of his infancy comes flooding back in the form of rain.[17] However, as the ominous title indicates, the book's principal focus is the apocalyptic catalogue of horrors that had besmirched the twentieth century, which the poet dolefully describes as an 'age of ashes'.[18] The Spanish Civil War, the Nazi camps, the US-led thwarting of independence movements in Africa and the ongoing war in Vietnam all loom large, precipitating moments of stark, bitter pessimism, as at the end of 'Siglo' ('Century'):

No nos hagamos ilusiones
nos aconseja el calendario,

Neruda as socialist icon on an East German stamp, issued on 22 January 1974.
The caption reads: 'I sound the storm bell of the victorious people.'

todo seguirá como sigue,
la tierra no tiene remedio:
en otras regiones celestes
hay que buscar alojamiento.[19]

Let's not fool ourselves
the calendar councils us,
everything will remain just as it is,
there's no curing this earth:
we'll have to look for accommodation
in other parts of the heavens.

Neruda's disgust sometimes catapults him into the sort of
unhinged rant that marred his poems about González Videla,
a prime example being the long, unstintingly vicious attack on
Portuguese dictator António Salazar, on whom he wishes a slow,
agonizing death. New causes for lament include pornography, the
degradations of which are bemoaned in the poem 'Sex' (the English

title suggesting that he views it primarily as an ugly excrescence of unfettered us capitalism) and that other promiscuity of the mass media ('Prensa' ['Press']), which threatens to engulf the world in a sea of lies and vulgar sensationalism. More pressing matters also require attention. For the first and only time in his poetry, Neruda alludes to the Russian invasion of Czechoslovakia, confessing in '1968' that 'La hora de Praga me cayó/como una piedra en la cabeza' ('The hour of Prague hit me/like a stone on the head').[20] Other political poems attack the personality cults of Stalin (who is belatedly named) and Mao, though even now Neruda thinks it acceptable to consign the past to oblivion and march on unabashed:

Luego es mejor el olvido
para sostener la esperanza.
[. . .]
La luz se descubrió
y recobramos la razón:
no por un hombre y su crimen
arrojaríamos el bien
a la bodega del malvado.[21]

So it is better to forget
if hope is to be sustained.
[. . .]
The light was revealed
and we recovered our reason:
we wouldn't throw good into the tyrant's hoard
for the sake of one man and his crime.

From such a description, one might imagine Stalin to have been no more than a petty crook. The same, only minimally troubled insistence on retrenchment also features in '1968':

Sufrimos de no defender
la flor que se nos amputaba
para salvar el árbol rojo
que necesita crecimiento.[22]

We suffered from not defending
the flower which we were having amputated
so as to save the red tree
which needs to grow.

Rehashing a jaded metaphor from the *Canto general* given a sinister
surgical twist, Neruda reiterates a depressingly familiar and utterly
dubious message: to make certain omelettes it is worth breaking
any number of eggs. One wonders what those being tortured in
Czech prisons or searching for the skeletons of loved ones in the
Gulag might have made of it. That mulish determination to battle
on at any cost causes him to end what, politically speaking, is
by far his darkest book, on a sudden upbeat note, which rings as
sickeningly hollow as the sudden blast of D major at the end of
Shostakovich's Fifth Symphony, while lacking any of the Russian
composer's irony:

A pesar de este fin de mundo
sobrevive el hombre infinito.
[. . .]
Encontraremos la alegría
en el planeta más amargo.[23]

Despite this world's end
infinite man survives
[. . .]
We shall find happiness
on this bitterest of planets.

Something akin to Beckett's 'I can't go on, I'll go on' might have been more apposite. Fortunately, there is more than jejune politicking to *Fin de mundo*. Poems such as the mock-philosophical meditation on time and identity, 'Metamorfosis' ('Metamorphosis'), and the animal poems 'Bestiario II' ('Bestiary II'), 'Perro' ('Dog') and 'Otro perro' ('Another Dog') contain flashes of the humour and whimsicality prevalent in *Estravagario*. Other animal poems, such as 'Bestiario I' ('Bestiary I') and 'Caballo' ('Horse') seek to reproduce the rapt splendour of 'Caballos' from the 1958 collection, though neither quite achieves it. Another highlight is the touching verse obituary for the madcap friend from his roistering Buenos Aires days, Oliverio Girondo, who had died in 1967. A second obituary, this time for Che Guevara ('Tristeza en la muerte de un héroe' ['Sadness on the Death of a Hero']), is notably more reserved and formulaic, perhaps because Neruda, as a senior Cold Warrior, simply felt obliged to pen an elegy for a man who may have been a global icon of the Left but whom he found both loutish and reckless (see chapter Six). Immediately preceding the poem to Che we find 'En Cuba' ('In Cuba'), an ebullient defence of the Revolution that includes his first poetic attack on the 'escribientes' ('scribblers') who signed the fateful letter of 1966. Another Cuban writer, José Lezama Lima (1910–1976), is subject to a merciless assault in one of a series of poems dedicated to contemporary Latin American novelists. With shocking homophobia, which might seem odd coming from a close friend of Lorca, but in fact was anything but untypical, Neruda repudiates him for being more interested in 'falos pegajosos' ('sticky phalluses') than in the ongoing Revolution.[24] How ironic, then, that Carlos Fuentes, Mario Vargas Llosa and Julio Cortázar, authors on whom he lavishes unqualified praise, should all have singled out Lezama's *Paradiso* (1966) as one of the pinnacles of twentieth-century Hispanic prose fiction, and that the book and its author should later have come to symbolize creative and sexual freedom in Cuba in Tomás Gutiérrez

Alea's film *Strawberry and Chocolate* (1993). The sequence itself is of negligible artistic worth, but it offers further evidence of that developing solidarity and sense of a common purpose – to 're-map' the continent in their works and attempt to unravel its complex history – shared by leading writers throughout Latin America in the 1960s. If, as Loyola and others claim, *Fin de mundo* was intended as another one of Neruda's large-scale, all-encompassing works, the 'last great journey through his experiences of history', it must be considered a failure, as it possesses far less overall coherence than either *Canto general* or *Memorial de Isla Negra*.[25] Viewed instead as a miscellany punctuated by a number of recurring themes, it is, like a great deal of his later poetry, a revealing, sporadically inspired but decidedly patchy work that would have benefited from some of the judicious pruning that had given such crispness and con-centrated eloquence to his early collections.

Even as Neruda was settling political scores on paper, flesh-and-blood politics dramatically re-entered his life after a hiatus of more than twenty years. In early September Luis Corvalán, Secretary General of the Chilean Communist Party, asked him to consider running for the presidency in the forthcoming national election. First, he would have to be selected from a group of four 'pre-candidates' put before the Unidad Popular, a potentially fractious, six-party leftist alliance. That meant another exhausting round of campaigning which, although by then he was almost certainly suffering from the cancer that would eventually kill him, he undertook with all the gusto he could muster. In the end, how-ever, it was not Neruda but Salvador Allende, who had fought and lost three previous elections (in 1952, 1958 and 1964), who was chosen. Yet if Neruda thought that Allende's nomination would allow him to withdraw from the fray and put his feet up at Isla Negra, he was very much mistaken.

8

A Final Flourish and a Last Defeat

The dawning of a new decade brought with it a familiar pendulum
swing in Neruda's life, from the high seriousness of national politics
to the soap opera-style melodrama of his personal affairs. In 1970
Matilde, who was fast approaching sixty and becoming obsessed
with her fading looks, decided to have plastic surgery in Buenos
Aires. Given her husband's condition – he was still morbidly obese,
at times almost immobile, and was suffering from a grave underlying
illness – she might have been forgiven for thinking that he could be
trusted during her absence. It turned out, however, that he could
not. While she was on the operating table, Neruda made a beeline
for her niece, Alicia, some thirty years his junior, who was staying
at Isla Negra. Their relationship, besides causing domestic havoc,
inspired a remarkable book, *La espada encendida* ('The Burning
Sword'). It takes the form of a secularized Genesis story, set in an
idealized Patagonia, involving, not surprisingly, an old man, Rhodo,
and a young woman, Rosía (perhaps a deformation of Rosario, the
name of Alicia's young daughter – even Neruda was sensitive
enough not to use the same fictional name for both aunt and niece),
who turn out to be the last earthly survivors of some unspecified
man-made disaster, very likely the nuclear holocaust grimly presaged
in poems such as the 'Oda al átomo' ('Ode to the Atom') and 'La
bomba I + II' ('The Bomb I + II') from *Fin de mundo*.[1] Adam and Eve
of a new, godless world, they fall passionately in love but, as in the
biblical story, they are driven out of their earthly paradise, in their

case by an erupting volcano. Now adopting the roles of Noah and his wife, they escape in an ark filled with birds and beasts, eventually landing on unknown shores where they must begin life anew by kindling fire, baking bread and peopling their brave new world. Here, with the future left open, the poem draws to a quiet close. In this final, muted scene, Rosía's praeternatural fertility – Rhodo says to her, 'Me darás cien hijos' ('You will bear me a hundred children') – stands in stark, even cruel contrast to Matilde's inability to have children. Besides being an amorous fantasy, the book is also a political parable, though its implication – that what currently passes off as mankind will have to be eradicated completely before true social justice is possible – is hardly an encouraging one. Neruda had written nothing like *La espada encendida* before, so how did he come up with the idea? In a brilliant piece of literary detective work, Hernán Loyola located his precise source of inspiration, a brief prose tale by French writer Marcel Schwob entitled *L'Incendie terrestre* ('The Earthly Conflagration'), which Neruda had translated for *Claridad* as long ago as 1923, and which tells a story almost identical to the one recounted in his own work. Whether the affair between Pablo and Alicia was ever consummated, or remained no more than an old man's wishful thinking, is unclear. Feinstein cites the torrid eroticism of the poetry as evidence that it was, but poets have a habit of putting into words exploits dreamt of rather than accomplished, and by then Neruda was suffering from prostate problems severe enough to have caused frequent bouts of impotence. Whatever the case, he remained intensely infatuated with Alicia for some time. Matilde quickly found out about the affair and reacted by throwing Alicia out of the house and threatening to leave Pablo. In an odd – or, in Neruda's case, perhaps not so odd – quirk of fate, it was radical politics that saved their marriage. On 4 September 1970, by the slimmest of majorities (just over 1 per cent of the vote), Salvador Allende became the world's first democratically elected Marxist president. Neruda, desperate to leave behind the mess at home, begged his old friend for a diplomatic posting as Ambassador to France. His request was granted and the Senate formally ratified the appointment in January 1971. Before setting off, he and Matilde visited Easter Island as part of a project to make a documentary, *Historia y geografía de Pablo Neruda* ('History and Geography of Pablo Neruda'), for Chilean television. The trip also resulted in a new book, *La rosa separada* ('The Separate Rose'), which was published the following year. This slim volume, which documents and muses over the poet's encounter with the ruins of a lost civilization, is most profitably viewed as a disenchanted revision of 'Alturas de Macchu Picchu'. In fact, Neruda may have borrowed the title, which alludes to the geographical isolation of the island, more than 3,200 km off the Chilean coast, from the earlier poem, though there the Inca citadel was described as 'la rosa *permanente*' ('the permanent rose'), an enduring link between past and present.[2] Neruda had dedicated a sequence of poems to Easter Island in 'El gran océano',

Celebrating the victory of the Unidad Popular with newly elected president Salvador Allende, 1970.

the penultimate section of the *Canto general*, and at least one of them, 'Los constructores de estatuas' ('The Statue Builders'), hints at the same sense of transhistorical continuity that he became aware of on the Andean heights.[3] Now, however, there is no epiphany, no feeling of elemental contact with a place suggestively known as 'the navel of the great ocean' in the native language. Instead, surrounded by a 'herd' of vulgar tourists (astonishingly, he dismisses them as 'proles'; that the Spanish word ['la prole' – 'the vulgar horde'] is not intended in a strictly political sense here hardly matters), he recognizes that an unbridgeable abyss separates the ancient civilization from the modern world; if it does represent some primordial fount of humanity, it is one from which contemporary man has been irretrievably severed. He briefly flatters himself that his peculiarly poetic awareness of the island's grandeur sets him apart from the camera-wielding crowd, but is soon forced to admit that he is no different from the rest:

> *No me sentí capaz sino de transitorios*
> *edificios, y en esa capital sin paredes*
> *hecha de luz, de sal, de piedra y pensamiento,*
> *como todos miré y abandoné asustado*
> *la limpia claridad de la mitología.*[4]

> I only felt able to cope with transitory
> buildings, and in that unwalled capital
> made of light, salt, stone and thought,
> like everyone else I looked upon and abandoned in fear
> the limpid clarity of mythology.

As it happens, had he returned to tourist-infested Machu Picchu in 1971, he would almost certainly have had the same disheartening experience. By then the lost Inca citadel had indeed become a 'fantastic place for a barbecue'. The sequence ends with the poet, like his fellow travellers a mere 'passer-by', returning to the daily grind, leaving the Moai staring inscrutably into space. The contrast with the triumphant Mosaic ascent of 1943 could scarcely be more pronounced.

By April the couple had settled in Paris. They were accompanied by Jorge Edwards, who had agreed to act as Neruda's official assistant but frequently found himself in the role of go-between, secretly handing over Alicia's letters from Chile. For a while Neruda even seems to have considered bringing her over to France, but soon far more urgent matters distracted him. Shortly after his arrival, Neruda had his first prostate operation. Apparently Matilde, but not the poet himself, was told that he had cancer. Accounts concerning Neruda's final illness are both puzzling and conflicting. Did he know how ill he was, and could his illness have been treated successfully? Some, like his doctor friend Francisco Velasco, claim that, after initial tests, Neruda had been too frightened to go back, a decision that proved fatal.[5] Matilde always maintained that Neruda never knew he had cancer. Apparently the doctors had told her that, if he avoided undue stress, he might live for many years, so she withheld the information. In his correspondence with Jorge Edwards he would commonly refer to his 'rheumatism', but some of his last poems clearly suggest that he knew the truth.[6] In an ironic piece about his officious doctors, he says:

Y con mi próstata melancólica
y los caprichos de mi uretra
me conducían sin apuro
a un analítico final.[7]

And with my melancholy prostate
and the whims of my urethra
they led me unhurriedly
to an analytical end.

The body parts have hardly been chosen at random. Just months later, while holidaying in Italy, he fainted and fell into a semi-coma. Somehow he recovered, just in time to learn that, after years of rumours, speculation and attempted sabotage, he had been awarded that year's Nobel Prize. The official announcement was made on 21 October, and in December he and Matilde travelled to Stockholm, where the prize-giving ceremony took place on 13 December. Despite the considerable unevenness of his vast output, particularly of the committed poetry, he was a worthy winner. He deserved the award for *Residencia en la tierra* alone, though ironically, given the strictly humanitarian remit of the prize (awarded for 'the most outstanding work of an idealistic tendency') that book scarcely merited a mention. Predictably, the judges singled out *Canto general*, 'poetry that with the action of an elemental force brings alive a continent's destiny and dreams.'[8] Neruda correspondingly dedicated much of his moving but occasionally fanciful acceptance speech (see chapter Four) to recounting his hazardous escape across the Andes in 1949. Shortly after receiving the prize, he headed for Moscow, where he received further medical treatment. Then it was back to France, where he celebrated the New Year at La Manquel (the Mapuche Indian word for 'condor'), a country retreat that he had purchased in Normandy with his winnings. The house was a converted slate mill of modest proportions, though right-wing political opponents back in Chile spread the word that the *soi-disant* communist Neruda was living like a lord in a French château.

During the early months of 1972 he made his final visits to Italy, where he attended the Thirteenth Congress of the Italian Communist Party, New York, where he spoke at a dinner on 10 April to celebrate the fiftieth anniversary of the founding of the PEN American Centre and gave two poetry recitals, and Moscow, where he had further emergency tests, but to no avail. In May *Geografía infructuosa* ('Barren Geography') appeared. Begun during his political campaign in Chile and completed in France, thematically and structurally

speaking it is one of Neruda's least unified books. This clearly
concerned him, as he appended an afterword detailing the often
chaotic circumstances of its composition. Despite this, it contains
some fine poems, especially 'El campanario de Authenay' ('The Bell
Tower at Authenay'), a much subtler, more restrained meditation
on Neruda's acutely felt incapacity to create anything truly lasting
than those of *Las manos del día*. Unsurprisingly, the inexorable
advance of time and the imminence of death cast a long shadow
over several poems – the bleak 'El cobarde' ('The Coward') is
perhaps the most haunting example – and Neruda's treatment
of these themes frequently recalls that of his beloved Quevedo,
whose presence, so important in his early work, is also perceptible
in much of his autumnal verse. In particular, his reference in
'Soliloquio inconcluso' ('Unfinished Soliloquy') to 'el hombre que
seré, que fui, que soy' ('the man I shall be, I was, I am') looks like
a conscious gloss of the famous line 'Soy un fue, y un será y un es
cansado' ('I am a was, a will be and an is tired') from Quevedo's
sonnet '¡Ah de la vida! ¿Nadie me responde?' ('Ho, Life! Is No One
There?'). The now remote past of his childhood is also a central
concern, occasionally re-emerging with memorable vividness,
such as when he recalls the muses who inspired his first poems:

Inextinguible, vivo mis besos más antiguos,
tengo aún en los labios un sabor
a luna llena errante, la más lejana, aquella
que viajaba en el cielo como una novia muerta
en la noche salvaje de Temuco.[9]

Inextinguishable, I live my oldest kisses,
I still have on my lips a taste
of wandering full moon, the most distant moon, the one
which journeyed across the sky like a dead bride
in the savage night of Temuco.

His health was now failing rapidly. A reporter at the Poetry International Festival in London, held in early June, described the poet, horribly bloated by steroids, as looking 'as sick as a beached whale', and after a further period in hospital later that month he underwent a second major operation in October.[10] All he wanted now was to return to Chile. When he got there, however, he found a very different country to the one he had left less than two years earlier. The Allende regime had been imperilled from the first. Ideological wrangling within the coalition made decision-making painfully difficult, and those sweeping social reforms that were approved, including the complete nationalization of foreign copper companies and most of the country's banks, provoked the ire of the United States. In fact, as part of its unstinting campaign against international socialism, the Nixon administration, which had been planning a coup against Allende even before his accession to the presidency, had begun an 'invisible blockade' against the Chilean economy as soon as he took up office, doing everything in its power to impede private foreign investment in the country. Inflation spiralled out of control, massive, often violent popular protests (both pro- and anti-Allende) became commonplace and a series of strikes further crippled an already enfeebled economy. The opposition, which controlled Congress, was predictably intransigent, meaning that the government, which acted in complete accordance with Chile's democratic constitution throughout, had almost no room to manoeuvre. Neruda's response to this dire situation was his angriest and for many his worst book, the dyspeptically titled *Incitación al nixonicidio y alabanza de la revolución chilena* ('Incitation to Nixoncide and Praise of the Chilean Revolution'). Written at breakneck speed during December 1972 and January 1973, it is an extreme *pièce d'occasion*, a work whose sole purpose was to whip up popular opposition to US meddling in national affairs and garner support for Allende in the imminent congressional elections. Aesthetic concerns could be jettisoned, as Neruda made abundantly clear in his foreword:

[This book] is neither concerned with nor strives for delicacy of expression, nor for the nuptial hermeticism of some of my metaphysical books ... I have no choice: against the enemies of my people my song is aggressive and hard as Araucanian stone. This may be an ephemeral objective, but I shall fulfil it. And I shall avail myself of poetry's most ancient weapons, the songs and pamphlets used by the Classicists and the Romantics designed to destroy the enemy. Now, watch out, because I'm about to fire![11]

There is nothing remotely delicate or hermetic about *Incitación al nixonicidio*, which consists of a barrage of rhymed insults and incriminations, sporadically leavened by a stanza or two in support of the Allende regime. Regardless of the exigencies of the moment, had it proved to be Neruda's final book it would have constituted a pitifully unworthy testament to his life's work. Fortunately, it did not, though no one could have predicted the remarkable cornucopia that was still to come.

In mid-1973 Neruda handed over to his publisher, Losada, no fewer than seven new books of poetry, one for every decade of his life, which he intended to have published the following year as part of his seventieth birthday celebrations. They turned out to be his poetic epitaph. As his readers had come to expect, they are extraordinarily varied. Some, such as *Jardín de invierno* ('Winter Garden'), are predominantly melancholy and introspective. This collection includes one of the greatest poems of Neruda's final period, the serene but profoundly affecting 'Con Quevedo, en primavera' ('With Quevedo, in Spring'), in which the gravely ill poet watches spring return as his own life reaches its winter:

Todo ha florecido en
estos campos, manzanos,
azules titubeantes, malezas amarillas,

y entre la hierba verde viven las amapolas,
el cielo inextinguible, el aire nuevo
de cada día, el tácito fulgor,
regalo de una extensa primavera.
Sólo no hay primavera en mi recinto.
Enfermedades, bocas desquiciadas,
como yedras de iglesias se pegaron
a las ventanas negras de mi vida
y el solo amor no basta, ni el salvaje
y extenso aroma de la primavera.[12]

Everything has blossomed in
these fields, apple trees,
swaying cornflowers, yellow thickets,
and amidst the green grass live the poppies,
the inextinguishable sky, the new air
of each day, the tacit gleam,
gift of a spreading spring.
Only where I dwell does Spring not come.
Illnesses, crazed mouths,
clung like church ivy
to the black windows of my life
and love alone is not enough, nor the wild
and pervasive aroma of Spring.

Note how Neruda uses enjambment as an organizing structural device throughout the poem to suggest time's even but ineluctable advance. *Jardín de invierno* closes with the brief, stark 'La estrella' ('The Star'), in which the poet stoically accepts that he is not going to recover from his illness.

Some of the other posthumous works, however, especially *Defectos escogidos* ('Selected Defects') and *El corazón amarillo* ('The Yellow Heart') are full of the self-deprecating humour that had been a mainstay of Neruda's poetry since *Estravagario*. Indeed the latter, written in the wake of his affair with Alicia, may well be a deliberate attempt to recapture the playful mood of the earlier collection, the first that he had written with Matilde as his official partner, and to which she herself had contributed. Certainly, the poem 'Integraciones' ('Integrations') looks like part of a strategy to woo her back.[13] *Libro de las preguntas* ('Book of Questions') meanwhile, consists of a series of no fewer than 317 questions, many of them touchingly childlike or plain absurd:

> *Dime, la rosa está desnuda,*
> *o sólo tiene ese vestido?*

> Tell me, is the rose naked,
> or is that her only dress?

> *Qué pensarán de mi sombrero*
> *en cien años, los polacos?*

> What, in a hundred years' time,
> will the Poles think of my hat?

> *Dónde termina el arco iris,*
> *en tu alma o en el horizonte?*[14]

> Where does the rainbow end,
> in your soul or on the horizon?

Others shift between poignant observation and quasi-philosophical inquiry:

> *Hay algo más triste en el mundo*
> *que un tren inmóvil en la lluvia?*

Is there anything more sad in the world
than a train motionless in the rain?

Sufre más el que espera siempre
Que aquel que nunca esperó a nadie?[15]

Does he who waits forever suffer more
than he who has never waited for anybody?

The first of these clearly springs from memories of his father in Temuco. He also breezily debunks his famous pseudonym, which still had the critics guessing:

Hay algo más tonto en la vida
que llamarse Pablo Neruda?[16]

Is there anything dafter in life
than being called [calling oneself] Pablo Neruda?

The rapid-fire question format constitutes yet another new formal departure, though it may owe something to the quirky *Greguerías* of Spanish surrealist poet Ramón Gómez de la Serna (1888–1963), whom Neruda had met in Spain in the 1930s and whose vast, breathtakingly inventive *oeuvre* he greatly admired.

2000 and *Elegía* ('Elegy') are slighter and less satisfying works. The first, consisting of just nine poems, picks up the apocalyptic thread of *Fin de mundo*, while the second focuses on Neruda's dealings with and thoughts on Russia, and on dead heroes and friends. Here again Lenin, the 'fragile constructor of greatness', is championed over Stalin 'the terrible', though even now the latter is portrayed as an essentially good man unaccountably gone bad:

Luego, adentro de Stalin,
entraron a vivir Dios y el Demonio,
se instalaron en su alma.
Aquel sagaz, tranquilo georgiano,
conocedor del vino y muchas cosas,
aquel capitán claro de su pueblo,
aceptó la mudanza.[17]

Then, within Stalin,
God and the Devil took up residence,
ensconcing themselves in his soul.
That shrewd, tranquil Georgian,
connoisseur of wine and so much else,
that shining captain of his people,
accepted the change.

Given what he knew by then, the disingenuousness of this account, which barely deserves to be called poetry, is truly jaw-dropping.

Perhaps the finest of the posthumous collections is *El mar y las campanas* ('The Sea and the Bells'), which was left unfinished on Neruda's death. The title refers to two of the most enduring symbols or presences in his *oeuvre*. Neruda has a claim to being the greatest poet of the sea in the Spanish language, while bells, which have unequivocally positive connotations – of joy, celebration, unfettered energy – clang throughout his work. As far back as the *Veinte poemas de amor* we find the youthful poet, bursting with desire, comparing himself to a 'campanario en manos de un loco' ('a bell tower in the hands of a madman'), while even the murk of *Residencia en la tierra* is occasionally lifted by euphoric peeling, as at the remarkable close of 'Entrada a la madera', where it erupts as if from nowhere:

Y hagamos fuego, y silencio, y sonido,
y ardamos, y callemos, y campanas.[18]

And let's make fire, and silence, and sound,
and let's burn, and be silent, and bells.

Now, unsurprisingly, the tone is more muted, and in 'Esta campana
rota' ('This Broken Bell') we find the poet, in a twilight reprise of
Baudelaire's 'La Cloche fêlée', comparing himself to a shattered
bell lying in his garden:

Esta campana rota
quiere sin embargo cantar:
el metal ahora es verde,
color de selva tiene la campana,
color de agua de estanques en el bosque,
color del día en las hojas.
[...]
Esta campana rota
arrastrada en el matorral
de mi jardín salvaje,
campana verde, herida,
hunde sus cicatrices en la hierba:
no llama a nadie más, no se congrega
junto a su copa verde
más que una mariposa que palpita
sobre el metal caído y vuela huyendo
con alas amarillas.[19]

This broken bell
still wants to sing:
the metal now is green,
the bell has the colour of the forest,
the colour of water in woodland pools,
the colour of the day on the leaves.
[...]

This broken bell
engulfed by the scrub
of my unruly garden,
this green, wounded bell,
sinks its scars into the grass:
it no longer calls out to anyone, no one gathers
around its green crown
other than a butterfly which flits
over the fallen metal and flies off
on yellow wings.

The limpid tranquillity of these lines, in which the poet, sombre but serene, acknowledges that life will continue indifferently without him, is typical of the finest poems in the book, which ends with a brief, touching love-song to Matilde:

Fue tan bello vivir
cuando vivías!

El mundo es más azul y más terrestre
de noche, cuando duermo
enorme, dentro de tus breves manos.[20]

It was so beautiful to live
while you were alive!

The world is more blue and more earthly
at night, when I lie asleep,
enormous, within your tiny hands.

While Neruda was in quietly valedictory mood at Isla Negra, the rest of the country was rapidly descending into chaos. On 29 June an attempted coup against Allende, the so-called 'tanquetazo', was

The bombing of La Moneda, Chile's presidential palace, during Augusto Pinochet's military coup of 11 September 1973.

crushed, but it was accompanied by a new wave of strikes (including a doctors' strike, which deprived Neruda of much needed palliative treatment) that left the country on the brink of collapse. Then, on 11 September, Allende was unseated by a second, far better co-ordinated coup, aggressively backed by the US and led by General Augusto Pinochet, whom he had named as his new chief of military staff just weeks before, believing him to be loyal to the regime. Allende, holed up in La Moneda, Chile's presidential palace, initially tried to resist but, under a hail of rocket fire and surrounded by rebel troops, chose to take his own life rather than surrendering. Three days later, a late-night military raid took place at Isla Negra. As the soldiers were rifling through drawers and cupboards, a bed-ridden Neruda turned to the officer in charge and said, 'Go ahead, look around, there's only one thing of danger to you here: poetry.' Ashamed, the young man removed his helmet and mumbled an apology. No damage was done to the house, though that was not the case at La Chascona, which was reduced to rubble in a similar operation. Fortunately, Neruda never found out. According to Matilde, the *coup d'état* destroyed Neruda's previously iron will to live. She insisted that he could have survived for years had the Allende government not fallen. Given the advanced state of his cancer, this is extremely doubtful, though no doubt this terrible blow, which brought about the demise of everything for which Neruda had struggled throughout the latter part of his life, hastened the end. He had just enough strength left to compose a final entry in his memoirs, in which he bitterly condemns the conspirators and praises his brave friend, whom he compares to the great Chilean president José Balmaceda who, at the end of the nineteenth century, had also tried to nationalize the country's natural resources and who had also ended up committing suicide after being ousted by a military uprising.[21] By 18 September, however, he was mortally ill, and Matilde had him hospitalized in Santiago. There he lasted just five more days, dying on Sunday 23 September at 10.30 p.m. He did not,

Crowds at Neruda's funeral in Santiago, 25 September 1973.

Neruda's final resting place at Isla Negra.

however, go gently. Two days later, as his coffin was being carried to General Cemetery, the cortège was joined by a group of students and workers. As they processed, shouts of 'Comrade Pablo Neruda!' were answered with the defiant reply 'Present!' Approaching the graveside, and surrounded by a ring of heavily armed soldiers, the mourners began to sing the 'Internationale', bellowing the words and punching the air with their fists. Then new cries were heard. First came 'Comrade Víctor Jara!' (a popular singer who had been viciously tortured and dispatched by Pinochet's henchmen just days after the coup, and who had sung in protest even as they thrashed him) and then, finally, 'Comrade Salvador Allende!', which, as Hernán Loyola remembers, was met with a 'hoarse, broken howl distorted by emotion and terror and the desire to shout it out so the whole world could hear: "Present!"'[22] Someone produced a copy of *España en el corazón* and recited the lines from 'Explico algunas cosas' in which the poet had condemned Franco's invasion of Spain:

Chacales que el chacal rechazaría
[…]
Generales
traidores:
mirad mi casa muerta,
mirad España rota.[23]

Jackals which the jackal itself would spurn,
[…]
Generals,
traitors:
look at my dead house,
look at shattered Spain.

From beyond the grave, Neruda had orchestrated the first popular protest against the new regime; nothing would have pleased him more. With the military in charge, his abiding wish to be buried at Isla Negra, by the sea that he so adored, could not be granted. Only after Pinochet's brutal, eighteen-year dictatorship had come to an end was his body finally transferred there in 1992. The grave, which he shares with Matilde, is washed by the spray of the Pacific waves.

References

oc: Pablo Neruda, *Obras completas*, ed. Hernán Loyola (Barcelona, 1999–2003)

Introduction

1 Jorge Luis Borges, *El hacedor* [1960] (Madrid, 1987), p. 155.
2 oc, v, p. 977. For details of the gondola chase see Adam Feinstein, *Pablo Neruda: A Passion for Life* (London, 2004), p. 259.
3 Jorge Luis Borges, 'Quevedo', in *Otras inquisiciones* [1952] (Madrid, 1985), p. 51.
4 oc, v, pp. 947, 1027.
5 oc, i, pp. 369–71, 383–5.
6 Isaiah Berlin, *The Hedgehog and the Fox: An Essay on Tolstoy's View of History* [1953] (London, 1999).
7 Nicanor Parra (with Pablo Neruda), *Discursos* (Santiago, 1962), p. 9.

1 From the Frontier to the Metropolis

1 oc, v, p. 406.
2 Bernardo Reyes, *Neruda: Retrato de familia, 1904–1920* (San Juan, Puerto Rico, 1996), pp. 24–52.
3 oc, v, pp. 402–3; 'La poesía' ('Poetry'), in oc, ii, pp. 1155–6.
4 oc, v, p. 400; oc, iv, p. 919. See also the wonderful 'Oda a la lluvia' ('Ode to Rain') in oc, ii, pp. 147–52.
5 oc, v, p. 428.
6 oc, ii, p. 1149.

7 Hernán Loyola, *Neruda: La biografía literaria* (Santiago, 2006), pp. 64–5.

8 *oc*, v, p. 427; *oc*, i, pp. 324–5.

9 *oc*, i, p. 351.

10 See for example 'Océano' ('Ocean'), 'Los nacimientos' ('Births') and 'La noche marina' ('Night at Sea'), in *oc*, i, pp. 643–4, 769–71, 803–6, and 'Oceana', in *oc*, ii, pp. 1075–9.

11 *oc*, ii, p. 695.

12 *oc*, iv, p. 165.

13 Reproduced in *oc*, iv, pp. 49–211.

14 *oc*, v, p. 495.

15 *oc*, iv, p. 925; see also 'Los libros' ('Books'), in *oc*, ii, p. 1169.

16 See especially 'La chair est triste, hélas!' (1920), in *oc*, iv, pp. 164–5.

17 See 'Ivresse', in *oc*, i, pp. 114–15 and the fifth entry from 'Álbum Terusa', in *oc*, iv, p. 274.

18 *oc*, v, p. 571.

19 Ibid., p. 1194.

20 Adam Feinstein, *Pablo Neruda: A Passion for Life* (London, 2004), p. 23.

21 Robertson Álvarez, 'Pablo Neruda: enigma inaugural', in *América sin nombre*, 1 (1999), pp. 50–64. The cover of the score is reproduced in Loyola, *Neruda: La biografía literaria*, p. 82.

22 Jason Wilson, *A Companion to Neruda: Evaluating Neruda's Poetry* (Woodbridge, 2008), pp. 14–17; Diego Muñoz, *Memorias: Recuerdos de la bohemia nerudiana* (Santiago, 1999), p. 22.

23 *oc*, ii, pp. 1171–2.

24 Tomás Lago, 'Pablo Neruda: Tras el rastro de un perfil', *Antártica*, 10–11 (June–July 1945), p. 30.

25 'Ausencia de Joaquín' ('Joaquín's Absence') and 'Alberto Rojas Giménez viene volando' ('Alberto Rojas Jimenez Comes Flying'), in *oc*, i, pp. 263, 335–8. The latter is perhaps Neruda's greatest elegiac poem.

26 *oc*, iv, pp. 260–61.

27 Ibid., pp. 252–6.

28 Edmundo Olivares Briones, *Tras las huellas de un poeta itinerante* (Santiago, 2000–2004), i, pp. 292–3.

29 Lago, 'Tras el rastro de un perfil', p. 34.

30 Rodolfo Rocker, 'Dictadura y socialismo', *Claridad*, 55 (10 June 1922), p. 7.

31 *oc*, v, pp. 424–6. For an account of his sexual exploits in Santiago, see Muñoz, *Memorias: Recuerdos de la bohemia nerudiana*.

32 *OC*, II, pp. 1180–81.

33 *OC*, V, p. 450. 'Farewell' was also Che Guevara's favourite Neruda poem. He apparently had his secretary draw up a handwritten copy which he took with him on his catastrophic African campaign of 1965.

34 Ibid., p. 929.

35 Ibid., p. 451.

36 Ibid., pp. 929–30.

37 *OC*, IV, p. 1201.

38 *OC*, V, pp. 451–2.

39 *OC*, V, p. 316; *OC*, IV, p. 1054.

40 *OC*, I, p. 179.

41 Ibid., p. 188.

42 Lago, 'Tras el rastro de un perfil', pp. 30–31.

43 *OC*, I, pp. 193–4.

44 See 'Hamlet', in *Selected Prose of T. S. Eliot* (London, 1954), pp. 45–9 (p. 48).

45 *OC*, V, p. 1150.

46 *OC*, I, p. 191.

47 Ibid., p. 95.

48 Ibid., p. 196.

49 *OC*, V, p. 453.

50 See *Veinte poemas de amor y una cancion desesperada*, ed. Dominic Moran (Manchester, 2007), pp. 14–18.

51 *OC*, IV, p. 1056.

52 Ibid., pp. 323–4.

53 *OC*, IV, p. 1085; *OC*, V, p. 237.

54 *OC*, I, p. 204.

55 Ibid., p. 161.

2 Residence on Earth

1 Robert Pring-Mill, *Pablo Neruda: A Basic Anthology* (Oxford, 1975), pp. xxi–xxii.

2 *OC*, V, p. 944.

3 *OC*, I, p. 157.

4 Hernán Loyola, *Neruda: La biografía literaria* (Santiago, 2006), pp. 232–36.

5 *OC*, v, p. 959.

6 Pring-Mill, *Pablo Neruda: A Basic Anthology*, p. xxii.

7 *OC*, v, pp. 487–8.

8 *OC*, i, p. 813; *OC*, ii, pp. 1199, 1231–2.

9 *OC*, v, pp. 939, 944, 946, 948.

10 Ibid., pp. 942, 1138.

11 Ibid., p. 470.

12 *OC*, ii, pp. 245–8, 650–51.

13 Reproduced in facsimile in Sergio Macías Brevis, *El Madrid de Pablo Neruda* (Madrid, 2004), p. 41.

14 Cited in Alfredo Cardona Peña, *Pablo Neruda y otros ensayos* (Mexico City, 1955), p. 30. De Torre's article was published in the Madrid newspaper *Luz* (17 August 1934).

15 *OC*, i, p. 292.

16 *OC*, v, p. 501.

17 *OC*, i, p. 345.

18 *OC*, i, pp. 274, 286–8, 319–20, 343–4, 313–14, 357–63; *OC*, ii, pp. 632–3, 664–5, 1233–8.

19 Loyola, *La biografía literaria*, pp. 411–12. More prosaically, but perhaps more plausibly, Jason Wilson suggests that he got the name 'Bliss' from his readings of Lawrence in Ceylon, and christened Josie retrospectively. See Jason Wilson, *A Companion to Neruda: Evaluating Neruda's Poetry* (Woodbridge, 2008), p. 121.

20 *OC*, v, p. 942.

21 Ibid., pp. 494–5.

22 *OC*, i, pp. 285–8.

23 *OC*, v, pp. 502–3.

24 For details see Adam Feinstein, *Pablo Neruda: A Passion for Life* (London, 2004), pp. 74–6.

25 *OC*, i, pp. 265–6, 293–4.

26 Ibid., pp. 314–16, 331–4.

27 *OC*, ii, pp. 686–9.

28 'Un perro ha muerto' ('A Dog Has Died'), in *OC*, iii, pp. 829–31.

29 See the letter to Sara Tornú in *OC*, v, p. 1029. For a full account of Neruda's relationship with his daughter see Bernardo Reyes, *Malva Marina: El enigma de la hija de Pablo Neruda* (Santiago, 2007).

30 Diego Muñoz, *Memorias: Recuerdos de la bohemia nerudiana* (Santiago, 1999), pp. 180–83.

31 Bernardo Reyes, *Neruda: Retrato de familia, 1904–1920* (San Juan, Puerto Rico, 1996), pp. 118–28.

32 *OC*, V, pp. 941, 1026.

33 *OC*, IV, p. 499.

3 Spain in the Heart

1 *OC*, V, pp. 924–6.

2 Reviews in *La Nación* (18 September 1932) and *El Mercurio* (11 September 1932).

3 *OC*, I, p. 185.

4 Ibid., p. 293.

5 *Residencia en la tierra*, ed. Hernán Loyola (Madrid, 1987), p. 42.

6 Review in *La Nación* (11 June 1933). For other early reactions see Edmundo Olivares Briones, *Tras las huellas de un poeta itinerante* (Santiago, 2000–2004), I, pp. 438–48.

7 *OC*, I, pp. 320–21.

8 The sole copy of this book was presented to Sara Tornú, wife of Argentine writer Pablo Rojas Paz, a mutual friend. It is reproduced in Pablo Neruda, *El fin del viaje: Obra póstuma* (Barcelona, 1982), pp. 101–43.

9 Federico García Lorca, *Poeta en Nueva York*, ed. María Clementa Millán (Madrid, 1987), pp. 161, 203–5; *OC*, I, pp. 309–11.

10 Indeed, the initially baffling allusions to sailor suits and masks in the poem 'Maternidad' (*OC*, I, p. 314) suggest that Neruda linked Maruca's pregnancy to one particularly extravagant revel, held to mark the publication of Norah Lange's *45 días y 30 marineros* ('45 days and 30 sailors'). A photo of this event can be found in Margarita Aguirre's *Las vidas del poeta* (Santiago, 1967), pp. 128–9.

11 Carlos Morla Lynch, *En España con Federico García Lorca* [1958] (Seville, 2008), p. 392.

12 This remarkable document is reproduced in Olivares, *Tras las huellas de un poeta itinerante*, II, pp. 242–4.

13 Federico García Lorca, *Obras completas*, III (Barcelona, 1997), p. 249.

14 Morla Lynch, *En España con Federico García Lorca*, p. 420.

15 Ibid., p. 471.

16 Ibid., p. 512.

17 Reproduced in *oc*, IV, pp. 374–80.

18 Throughout his life Neruda managed to make enough literary enemies, both in Chile (where he managed to alienate most of the major
poets, from Huidobro and De Rokha to surrealist Braulio Arenas and
his 'Mandrágora' group to fellow political poet Enrique Lihn) and
abroad, to fill an entire book of diatribes, slights and slurs. See
Leonardo Sanhueza, ed., *El bacalao: Diatribas antinerudianas y otros
textos* (Santiago, 2004).

19 Fernando Sáez, *Todo debe ser demasiado: Vida de Delia del Carril*
(Santiago, 1997), *passim*.

20 *oc*, I, p. 369.

21 Ibid., p. 343.

22 Ibid., p. 370.

23 Ibid., p. 371.

24 Robert Pring-Mill, *Pablo Neruda: A Basic Anthology* (Oxford, 1975),
p. xxvii.

25 *oc*, V, pp. 544–5.

26 Amado Alonso, *Poesía y estilo de Pablo Neruda* [1940] (Madrid, 1997),
p. 359.

27 *oc*, V, p. 967; Olivares, *Tras las huellas de un poeta itinerante*, II,
p. 195.

28 Gerald Brenan, *The Spanish Labyrinth* [1943] (Cambridge, 2006),
p. 284; Raúl González Tuñón, *La rosa blindada* [1935] (Buenos Aires,
1963), p. 32.

29 Cited in Adam Feinstein, *Pablo Neruda: A Passion for Life* (London,
2004), p. 108.

30 *Residencia en la tierra*, ed. Loyola, p. 58 (n. 20).

31 Abraham Quezada Vergara, ed., *Epistolario viajero, 1927–1973*
(Santiago, 2004), p. 119.

32 'Viaje al corazón de Quevedo' ('Journey to the Heart of Quevedo'),
in *oc*, IV, pp. 451–69. In Spain Neruda also put together an anthology
of Quevedo's poetry and prose, *Quevedo: Cartas y sonetos de la muerte*
(Madrid, 1935).

33 Carlos Morla Lynch, *España sufre: Diarios de Guerra en el Madrid
republicano* (Seville, 2008), p. 103.

34 *oc*, V, pp. 976–7.

35 *oc*, I, p. 586.

4 A Vision of America

1 *OC*, V, p. 1059.
2 Ibid., pp. 532–3.
3 *OC*, IV, pp. 929–31.
4 *OC*, I, pp. 829–30.
5 For a full account see Adam Feinstein, *Pablo Neruda: A Passion for Life* (London, 2004), pp. 130–49.
6 *OC*, V, p. 247.
7 *OC*, II, p. 1274.
8 See for example 'México', 'En los muros de México' ('On the Walls of Mexico') and 'Serenata de México' ('Mexican Serenade'), in *OC*, I, pp. 818–22 and *OC*, II, pp. 1280–85.
9 *El laberinto de la soledad* [1950], ed. Enrico Mario Santí (Madrid, 1998), p. 293.
10 Hugo Méndez-Ramírez, *Neruda's Ekphrastic Experience: Mural Art and Canto general* (Lewisburg, PA, 2000).
11 Rafael Alberti, *La arboleda perdida* (Madrid, 1998), II, p. 116.
12 See Octavio Paz, 'Poesía e historia (*Laurel* y nosotros)', in *Sombras de obras* (Barcelona, 1983), pp. 47–94 (pp. 51–6). The dates are somewhat hazy here, as in an interview with Mexican newspaper *El Excelsior* on 7 December 1990, Paz claimed that the fateful dinner took place in 1942. This is also the date quoted by Feinstein and others.
13 Octavio Paz, 'Respuesta a un cónsul', in *Letras de Mexico* (15 August 1943).
14 *OC*, I, p. 396.
15 *El Siglo* (27 November 1944).
16 *OC*, I, p. 410.
17 *OC*, IV, p. 483.
18 Feinstein, *Pablo Neruda: A Passion for Life*, p. 174.
19 *OC*, IV, p. 932.
20 *OC*, I, p. 434.
21 Ibid., p. 435.
22 Ibid., p. 439.
23 Ibid., p. 365.
24 Enrico Mario Santí, *Pablo Neruda: The Poetics of Prophecy* (Ithaca, NY, 1982), pp. 166–7.

25 *OC*, I, p. 447.

26 Ibid., p. 430.

27 *OC*, IV, pp. 541–5, 560–79.

28 *OC*, I, p. 357.

29 *OC*, IV, pp. 681–703.

30 Ibid., pp. 704–29.

31 Gabriel González Videla, *Memorias* (Santiago, 1975), I, pp. 761–2.

32 José Miguel Varas, *Neruda clandestino* (Santiago, 2003), pp. 188, 194.

33 For details see ibid., pp. 219–26.

34 *OC*, I, p. 417.

35 Rubén Darío, *Poesías completas* (Madrid, 1967), II, pp. 631–2, 639–41.

36 Enrico Mario Santí, 'Neruda: La modalidad apocalíptica', *Hispanic Review*, XLVI (1978), pp. 365–84 (p. 366).

37 *OC*, I, p. 687.

38 Ibid., pp. 833–4.

39 Ibid., p. 479.

40 For a summary of the critical reactions, see Olivares, *Tras las huellas de un poeta itinerante*, III, pp. 761–4.

41 Tomás Lago, *Ojos y oídos: Cerca de Neruda* (Santiago, 1999), pp. 114–15.

42 *OC*, I, p. 625.

43 Ibid., p. 623.

44 Ibid., pp. 640–43.

45 Ibid., p. 835.

46 *OC*, IV, p. 1205.

47 *Canto general*, ed. Enrico Mario Santí (Madrid, 1998), p. 94.

48 Julio Cortázar, with Oscar Collazos and Mario Vargas Llosa, *Literatura en la revolución y revolución en la literatura* (Mexico City, 1970), pp. 38–77.

49 Julio Cortázar, 'Carta abierta a Pablo Neruda', in *Pablo Neruda*, ed. Emir Rodríguez Monegal and Enrico Mario Santí (Madrid, 1980), pp. 31–6; 'Neruda entre nostoros', *Plural*, 30 (March 1974), pp. 38–41. The first of these appeared as a foreword to a 1972 French edition of *Residencia*. Fascinatingly, in a note recently published in Spanish for the first time, Cortázar intimates that, despite his public rejection of the work, to the very end of his life Neruda retained a private 'nocturnal fidelity' to his great early collection. See 'De una amistad' ('About a Friendship'), in Julio Cortázar, *Papeles inesperados* (Madrid, 2009), pp. 382–4 (p. 384).

50 Paz, *Sombras de obras*, pp. 84–5.

5 Love and Politics

1 Adam Feinstein, *Pablo Neruda: A Passion for Life* (London, 2004), p. 242.
2 *OC*, IV, pp. 761–9.
3 Bernardo Reyes, *Neruda: Retrato de familia, 1904–1920* (San Juan, Puerto Rico, 1996), p. 243.
4 *OC*, I, p. 699.
5 See Sergio Gómez's damning article 'Maldición eterna a quien lea estas páginas' ('An Eternal Curse on Whoever Reads These Pages') in the Buenos Aires newspaper *Página 12* (28 July 2002).
6 *OC*, I, p. 857.
7 Ibid., pp. 863–4.
8 Ibid., p. 869.
9 Ibid., pp. 883–5.
10 For a summary of their reactions, see Feinstein, *Pablo Neruda: A Passion for Life*, pp. 303–4.
11 *OC*, I, pp. 998–1004.
12 Pedro Gutiérrez Revuelta and Manuel Guriérrez, eds, *Pablo Neruda: Yo respondo con mi obra* (Salamanca, 2004), p. 222.
13 *OC*, V, pp. 725–6.
14 Mario Vargas Llosa, *La orgía perpetua: Flaubert y Madame Bovary* [1975] (Madrid, 2006), pp. 224–8.
15 *OC*, II, pp. 39–45.
16 Ibid., p. 48.
17 See for example the odes to the building, the sea, to bread and to spring (*OC*, II, pp. 88–90, 157–61, 182–5, 205–9).
18 Ibid., pp. 72–3.
19 *OC*, II, pp. 82–4, 142–4.
20 Fine examples of non-political odes include the haunting 'Oda a un reloj en la noche' ('Ode to a Watch in the Night') and the delightfully anti-Stakhanovite 'Oda a la pereza' ('Ode to Laziness') (*OC*, II, pp. 209–12, 192–4).
21 *OC*, IV, pp. 914–55.
22 Ibid., p. 931.

6 Crimes and Compromises

1 *OC*, II, pp. 491–4.
2 Ibid., p. 800.
3 *OC*, V, pp. 1201–2.
4 Ibid., p. 753.
5 *OC*, II, p. 1396.
6 Ibid.
7 Ibid., p. 1307.
8 *OC*, IV, p. 790.
9 *OC*, V, p. 1165.
10 Ibid., p. 654.
11 *OC*, II, p. 664.
12 *El Siglo* (30 September 1963), reproduced in Adam Feinstein, *Pablo Neruda: A Passion for Life* (London, 2004), p. 336.
13 *OC*, II, pp. 715–17, 628–9, 635–6.
14 Ibid., pp. 726–30, 653–4.
15 Ibid., pp. 666–8.
16 Ibid., pp. 651–3, 709–10, 657–8.
17 Ibid., pp. 665–6.
18 Ibid., p. 645.
19 Ibid., pp. 654–5.
20 Ibid., pp. 637–8.
21 Ibid., pp. 648–50, 668–70, 693–4.
22 Ibid., pp. 694–6.
23 Ibid., pp. 705–7.
24 Feinstein, *Pablo Neruda: A Passion for Life*, p. 326.
25 *OC*, II, pp. 939–40.
26 Ibid., p. 971.
27 Ariel Dorfman, 'Saying Goodbye to Pablo', in *Other Septembers, Many Americas* (London, 2004), pp. 158–9.
28 *OC*, II, p. 1091.
29 Ibid.
30 Ibid., pp. 1092–4, 1102–3, 1125–7.
31 Ibid., pp. 1116–18.
32 Ibid., pp. 1133–7.
33 Ibid., pp. 1141–3, 1144–7, 1151–2, 1152–5, 1148–51, 1160.
34 Ibid., p. 1156.

35 Ibid., pp. 1173–9, 1186–92, 1195–7.

36 Ibid., pp. 1218–19.

37 Ibid., pp. 1220–26, 1227–8, 1230–31, 1239.

38 *oc*, I, pp. 354–6.

39 *oc*, II, pp. 1261–2.

40 *oc*, I, pp. 257–8.

41 *oc*, II, pp. 1271–5.

42 *oc*, II, p. 1329.

43 *oc*, V, pp. 87, 97.

7 A Cuban Missile

1 *oc*, II, p. 973.

2 *oc*, I, p. 192. See also Poem 12 and the 'Song of Despair'.

3 *oc*, IV, p. 1116. See also the poems 'Oda a las aves de Chile' ('Ode to the
Birds of Chile'), 'Oda a mirar pájaros' ('Ode to Watching Birds'), 'Oda
a la gaviota' ('Ode to the Seagull') and 'Oda a la picaflor' ('Ode to the
Hummingbird') in *oc*, II, pp. 65–8, 162–6, 328–31, 368–71.

4 Jorge Edwards, *Adiós poeta* (Barcelona, 2004), p. 251.

5 Octavio Paz, *Obras completas* (Mexico City, 2003), XV, pp. 335–6. Paz
refers to Neruda as his 'dearest enemy' in 'Pablo Neruda (1904–1973)',
a touching commemorative piece published in *Vuelta*, no. 202
(September 1993).

6 Gabriel García Márquez, *Doce cuentos peregrinos* (Madrid, 1992),
pp. 93–101 (p. 98).

7 Esther Tusquets, 'Una tarde con Neruda en la Barcelona franquista',
El País (24 July 2004).

8 Rubén Darió, *Poesías completas* (Madrid, 1967), II, p. 627.

9 *oc*, V, pp. 1013–14.

10 Interview with Enrique Bello, in *oc*, V, pp. 1084–93 (p. 1085).

11 *oc*, III, p. 339.

12 *oc*, II, pp. 144–7.

13 Adam Feinstein, *Pablo Neruda: A Passion for Life* (London, 2004), p. 359.

14 *oc*, III, p. 369.

15 Ibid., p. 362.

16 *oc*, I, p. 206.

17 *oc*, III, p. 468; *oc*, I, pp. 324–43.

18 *oc*, III, p. 405.

19 Ibid., p. 459.

20 Ibid., p. 402.

21 Ibid., p. 462.

22 Ibid., p. 402.

23 Ibid., p. 509.

24 Ibid., p. 493. For a further example see 'Oda a la sencillez' ('Ode to Simplicity'), in *oc*, II, pp. 217–20 (p. 218).

25 Carlos Monsiváis, prologue to *Fin de mundo* (Barcelona, 2004), p. 7.

8 A Final Flourish and a Last Defeat

1 *oc*, II, pp. 60–64; *oc*, III, pp. 454–6, 472.

2 *oc*, I, p. 440.

3 Ibid., pp. 774–6.

4 *oc*, III, p. 700.

5 Adam Feinstein, *Pablo Neruda: A Passion for Life* (London, 2004), pp. 373–4.

6 Abraham Quezada Vergara, *Correspondencia entre Pablo Neruda y Jorge Edwards* (Santiago, 2008), p. 115.

7 *oc*, III, p. 788.

8 For the presentation speech go to http://nobelprize.org/nobel_prizes/ literature/laureates/1971/press.html.

9 *oc*, III, p. 675.

10 *The Guardian Weekly* (3 June 1972).

11 *oc*, III, pp. 706–7.

12 Ibid., p. 816.

13 Ibid., p. 794.

14 Ibid., pp. 836, 839, 855.

15 Ibid., pp. 836, 855.

16 Ibid., p. 850.

17 Ibid., p. 774.

18 *oc*, I, pp. 189, 325.

19 *oc*, III, p. 923. This poem might fruitfully be compared to the earlier 'Oda a la campana caída' ('Ode to the Fallen Bell') from *Navegaciones sy regresos* (*oc*, II, pp. 761–3).

20 Ibid., p. 940.

21 *OC*, V, pp. 785–9.
22 Cited in Feinstein, *Pablo Neruda: A Passion For Life*, pp. 419–20.
23 *OC*, I, pp. 370–71.

Select Bibliography

First Editions of Neruda's Poetry in Spanish

Crepusculario (Santiago, 1923)
Veinte poemas de amor y una canción desesperada (Santiago, 1924)
Tentativa del hombre infinito (Santiago, 1926)
El hondero entusiasta (Santiago, 1933)
Residencia en la tierra, I–II (Madrid, 1935)
España en el corazón (Santiago, 1938)
Tercera residencia (Buenos Aires, 1947)
Canto general (Mexico City, 1950)
Los versos del capitán (Naples, 1952)
Las uvas y el viento (Santiago, 1954)
Odas elementales (Buenos Aires, 1954)
Nuevas odas elementales (Buenos Aires, 1956)
Tercer libro de las odas (Buenos Aires, 1957)
Estravagario (Buenos Aires, 1958)
Navegaciones y regresos (Buenos Aires, 1959)
Cien sonetos de amor (Santiago, 1959)
Canción de gesta (Havana, 1960)
Las piedras de Chile (Buenos Aires, 1961)
Cantos ceremoniales (Buenos Aires, 1961)
Plenos poderes (Buenos Aires, 1962)
Memorial de Isla Negra (Buenos Aires, 1964)
Arte de pájaros (Santiago, 1966)
La barcarola (Buenos Aires, 1967)
Las manos del día (Buenos Aires, 1968)
Fin de mundo (Santiago, 1969)
Aún (Santiago, 1969)

Maremoto (Santiago, 1970)
La espada encendida (Buenos Aires, 1970)
Las piedras del cielo (Buenos Aires, 1970)
Geografía infructuosa (Buenos Aires, 1972)
La rosa separada (Paris, 1972)
Incitación al nixoncidio y alabanza de la revolución chilena (Santiago, 1973)
2000 (Buenos Aires, 1974)
Elegía (Buenos Aires, 1974)
El corazón amarillo (Buenos Aires, 1974)
Jardín de invierno (Buenos Aires, 1974)
Libro de las preguntas (Buenos Aires, 1974)
Defectos escogidos (Buenos Aires, 1974)
El mar y las campanas (Buenos Aires, 1974)

First Editions of Other Works by Neruda in Spanish

Anillos (Santiago, 1926, co-authored with Tomás Lago) [prose poems]
El habitante y su esperanza (Santiago, 1926) [novella]
Fulgor y muerte de Joaquín Murieta (Santiago, 1967) [play]
Confieso que he vivido: Memorias (Buenos Aires, 1974) [memoirs]

Works by Neruda in English (Selection)

Individual Poetry Collections

Works are listed in the order in which they originally appeared in Spanish.

Twenty Love Poems and a Song of Despair, trans. W. S. Merwin and Cristina
     García (London, 2006)
Residence on Earth and *Third Residence*, trans. Donald Walsh (London,
     1976) [includes *Spain in Our Hearts*]
Canto general, trans. Jack Schmitt (Berkeley, CA, 2000)
The Captain's Verses, trans. Brian Cole (London, 1994)
Selected Odes of Pablo Neruda, trans. Margaret Sayers Peden (Berkeley, CA,
     1990)

Extravagaria, trans. Alistair Reid (New York, 1974)
One Hundred Love Sonnets, trans. Stephen Trapscott (Austin, TX, 1986)
Song of Protest (Canción de gesta), trans. Miguel Algarín (New York, 1976)
Ceremonial Songs, trans. Maria Jacketti (Pittsburgh, PA, 1996)
Fully Empowered, trans. Alistair Reid (New York, 1975)
Isla Negra, trans. Alistair Reid (New York, 1981)
The Hands of the Day, trans. William O'Daly (Port Townsend, WA, 2008)
World's End, trans. William O'Daly (Port Townsend, WA, 2008)
The Separate Rose, trans. William O'Daly (Port Townsend, WA, 1985)
Incitement to Nixonicide and Praise for the Chilean Revolution, trans. Steve
	Kowitt (Wever, IA, 1980)
Elegy, trans. Jack Hirschman (San Francisco, CA, 1983)
Winter Garden, trans. William O'Daly (Port Townsend, WA, 1986)
The Yellow Heart, trans. William O'Daly (Port Townsend, WA, 1990)
The Book of Questions, trans. William O'Daly (Port Townsend, WA, 1991)
The Sea and the Bells, trans. William O'Daly (Port Townsend, WA, 1988)

Anthologies

Selected Poems, trans. Anthony Kerrigan (London, 1992)
Five Decades: Poems 1925–1970, trans. Ben Belitt (New York, 1994)
Late and Posthumous Poems, 1968–1974, trans. Ben Belitt (New York, 1994)
Full Woman, Fleshy Apple, Hot Moon: Selected Poems of Pablo Neruda, trans.
	Stephen Mitchell (New York, 1997)
The Poetry of Pablo Neruda, various translators, ed. Ilan Stavans (New York,
	2003)
The Essential Neruda: Selected Poems, various translators (London, 2004)
On the Blue Shore of Silence: Poems of the Sea, trans. Alistair Reid (New
	York, 2004)
Intimacies: Poems of Love, trans. Alistair Reid (New York, 2008)

Other Works

Memoirs, trans. Hardie St Martin (London, 1977)

Critical Works on Neruda

Biographical Works

Aguirre, Margarita, *Pablo Neruda: Las vidas del poeta* (Santiago, 1967)

Cardone, Inés María, *Los amores de Neruda* (Santiago, 2003)

Edwards, Jorge, *Adiós poeta* (Barcelona, 2004)

Feinstein, Adam, *Pablo Neruda: A Passion for Life* (London, 2004)

Gálvez Barraza, Julio, *Neruda y España* (Santiago, 2003)

Gutiérrez Revuelta, Pedro, and Manuel Gutiérrez, eds, *Pablo Neruda: Yo respondo con mi obra* (Salamanca, 2004)

Lago, Tomás, *Ojos y oídos: Cerca de Neruda* (Santiago, 1999)

Loyola, Hernán, *Neruda: La biografía literaria* (Santiago, 2006)

Macías Brevis, Sergio, *El Madrid de Pablo Neruda* (Madrid, 2004)

Muñoz, Diego, *Memorias: Recuerdos de la bohemia nerudiana* (Santiago, 1999)

Olivares Briones, Edmundo, *Tras las huellas de un poeta itinerante*, 3 vols (Santiago, 2000–2004)

Pring-Mill, Robert, 'Introduction' to *Pablo Neruda: A Basic Anthology* (Oxford, 1975)

Quezada Vergara, Abraham, ed., *Epistolario viajero, 1927–1973* (Santiago, 2004)

—, *Correspondencia entre Pablo Neruda y Jorge Edwards* (Santiago, 2008)

Reyes, Bernardo, *Neruda: Retrato de familia, 1904–1920* (San Juan, Puerto Rico, 1996)

—, *Malva Marina: El enigma de la hija de Pablo Neruda* (Santiago, 2007)

Sáez, Fernando, *Todo debe ser demasiado: Vida de Delia del Carril* (Santiago, 1997)

Schidlowsky, David, *Las furias y las penas: Pablo Neruda y su tiempo*, 2 vols (Berlin, 2003)

Teitelboim, Volodia, *Neruda: La biografía* (Santiago, 2003)

Urrutia, Matilde, *Mi vida junto a Pablo Neruda* (Barcelona, 1987)

Varas, José Miguel, *Neruda clandestino* (Santiago, 2003)

Vargas Llosa, Mario, 'Neruda at a Hundred', in *Touchstones*, trans. John King (London, 2007), pp. 126–30

Other

Alonso, Amado, *Poesía y estilo de Pablo Neruda* [1940] (Madrid, 1997).

Bloom, Harold, ed., *Pablo Neruda* (New York, 1989)

Brotherston, Gordon, *Latin American Poetry: Origins and Presence* (Cambridge, 1975), especially chapters 3 and 6

De Costa, René, *The Poetry of Pablo Neruda* (Cambridge, MA, 1979)

Felstiner, John, *Translating Neruda: The Way to Macchu Picchu* (Stanford, CA, 1980)

Loyola, Hernán, *Ser y morir en Pablo Neruda, 1918–1945* (Santiago, 1967)

Méndez-Ramírez, Hugo, *Neruda's Ekphrastic Experience: Mural Art and Canto General* (Lewisburg, PA, 2000)

Perriam, Christopher, *The Late Poetry of Pablo Neruda* (Oxford, 1989)

Reiss, Frank, *The Word and the Stone: Language and Imagery in Neruda's 'Canto general'* (Oxford, 1972)

Rodríguez Monegal, Emir, *El viajero inmóvil* [1966] (Barcelona, 1988)

Rodríguez Monegal, Emir, and Enrico Mario Santí, eds, *Pablo Neruda* (Madrid, 1980)

Rosales, Luis, *La poesía de Neruda* (Madrid, 1978)

Sanhueza, Leonardo, ed., *El bacalao: Diatribas antinerudianas y otros textos* (Santiago, 2004)

Santí, Enrico Mario, *Pablo Neruda: The Poetics of Prophecy* (Ithaca, NY, 1982)

Sicard, Alain, *El pensamiento poético de Pablo Neruda* (Madrid, 1981)

Silva Castro, Raúl, *Pablo Neruda* (Santiago, 1964)

Stavans, Ilan, *The Poetry of Pablo Neruda* (New York, 2003)

Suárez, Eulogio, *Neruda total* (Bogotá, 1988)

Wilson, Jason, *A Companion to Neruda: Evaluating Neruda's Poetry* (Woodbridge, 2008)

Yurkievitch, Saúl, *Fundadores de la nueva poesía hispanoamericana* (Barcelona, 1984), especially chapter 5

Acknowledgements

I would like to thank to my colleagues, students and friends at Oxford who, in seminars, tutorials, and conversation have contributed in numerous ways to the creation of this volume, but especially Clive Griffin and Eric Southworth, whose comments, criticisms and queries have, as ever, proved invaluable. I am also grateful to Denis Moran and Katherine Lunn-Rockliffe, who ploughed uncomplainingly through bloated early drafts of the text, to Jason Wilson for reading and correcting the original typescript and to Adam Feinstein for his various helpful suggestions. The gaffs and infelicities that remain are all my own. I would also like to thank the Fundación Pablo Neruda in Santiago for granting permission to reproduce the extracts of poetry cited in the text and Darío Oses for his help in securing that permission. Thanks too to Carolina Briones and Andrés Grillo at the Fundación for helping me sift through and select photographic material, and to Susannah Jayes for locating and obtaining permission to use many of the other illustrations. Last but by no means least, a word of gratitude goes to Vivian Constantinopoulos and the staff at Reaktion Books for their hard work, encouragement and, latterly, patience during the preparation of this book.

Photo Acknowledgements

The author and publishers wish to express their thanks to the following sources for illustrative material and/or permission to reproduce it:

Photo © Corbis: p. 194 (Bettmann); image courtesy of the Fundación Federico García Lorca: p. 70; photos courtesy of the Fundación Pablo Neruda: pp. 18, 22, 37, 58, 62, 67, 75, 80, 95, 103, 107, 129, 160, 163, 195; photo © Istockphoto: p. 100; photo courtesy of the Library of Congress: p. 29; photo courtesy of Mark Andrew Low: p. 87; photo courtesy of Francisco Martins (www.flickr.com/photos/betta): p. 196; photo courtesy of Bridget Pring-Mill: p. 161; photo © Rex Features: p. 6 (Roger-Viollet); photos courtesy of the Taylor Institute, University of Oxford: pp. 114–15; photo © Topfoto: p. 181 (Ullsteinbild).